ON THE CUTTING EDGE

THE BILL SUBRITZKY STORY

as told to Vic Francis

Sovereign World

Sovereign World Ltd
PO Box 777
Tonbridge
Kent TN11 9XT

Paperback ISBN: 1 85240 107 9
Hardback ISBN: 1 85240 131 1

Printed in England by Clays Ltd, St Ives plc.

DEDICATION

To my dear wife Pat,
who has been such a faithful helpmate
over many years

OTHER BOOKS BY BILL AND PAT SUBRITZKY

Demons Defeated
Receiving The Gifts of the Holy Spirit
How to Receive the Baptism with the Holy Spirit
How to Know the Anointing of God
How to be Born Again
Ministering in the Power of the Holy Spirit
But I Don't Believe in Miracles!
How to Overcome Fear
How to Cast out Demons and Break Curses
Miracle at Dubbo
How to Grow in Jesus (Books 1, 2 and 3)
How to Read your Bible in One Year
Chosen Destiny – The Pat Subritzky Story

VHS VIDEOS AND AUDIO CASSETTES

Crusade Miracles .... (25 mins)
The Bill Subritzky Story .... (55 mins)
How to be an Overcomer .... (48 mins)
Who is this Jesus? .... (55 mins)
Sons of the Kingdom .... (55 mins)
Fear or Faith? .... (55 mins)
The Fatal Choice .... (55 mins)
The Living God .... (55 mins)
Receiving God's Peace .... (45 mins)
Overcoming Fear .... (54 mins)
The Living Water .... (55 mins)
Finding the Doorway to God .... (49 mins)
Binding the Strong Men .... (55 mins)
What is Truth? .... (48 mins)
Thirsty People .... (45 mins)
Healed! .... (49 mins)
Behold the Man! .... (51 mins)
Chosen Destiny — the Pat Subritzky Story .... (23 mins)
Healing Marriages and Family Relationships .... (90 mins)
Hindrances to Healing .... (90 mins)
Receiving the Gifts of the Holy Spirit .... (4 hours)
Deliverance from Demons (New Version) .... (5 hours)
Ministering in the Power of the Holy Spirit
(plus Seminar Manual) .... (5 hours)
Christian Women Today Seminar .... (3.5 hours)
Exposing the New Age Movement (seminar for women) .... (4.5 hours)

FOR UPDATED CATALOGUE AND PRICE-LIST WRITE TO:

Dove Ministries, PO Box 48036 Blockhouse Bay, Auckland 7, NZ or:
Australia: Family Reading, 3 College St, Wendouree, Vic. 3355
UK: New Wine Ministries, PO Box 17 Chichester, West Sussex PO206YB
USA: Grace Distributors Inc. PO Box 39206 Denver, CO 80239-0206

Contents

Foreword

By HM *King Taufa'ahau Tupou* IV, *King of Tonga*

I am very happy to write this foreword to the biography of my friend, Bill Subritzky, whom I have known for many years. I know that he is filled, inspired and guided by the Holy Spirit of God and that he is working all the time to ensure that the gifts of the same Holy Spirit enrich the lives of fellow Christians and to bring those not yet in the fold to know Christ as their Saviour and Lord.

HM. King Taufa'ahau Tupou IV, Kingdom of Tonga

Foreword

By Derek Prince

I have enjoyed a close personal friendship with Bill and Pat Subritzky for many years. I have often been a guest in their home. I have seen their private lives as well as their public ministry. I can testify that they are just the same in private as they are in public — devoted servants of Jesus Christ.

Jesus said that "the tree is known by its fruit". Since Bill came to know Christ as his personal Saviour, he has been instrumental in the salvation of his family, as well as all four of their spouses. The whole family stands united in commitment to Jesus Christ.

Bill has developed one of the most powerful evangelistic ministries that it has been my privilege to witness at first-hand. His ministry is regularly attested by many miracles of healing and deliverance. More important still, he presents the Gospel in a clear, simple, uncompromising way that demands whole-hearted repentance from sin in all its forms and unreserved commitment to the lordship of Jesus Christ.

I pray that this book will extend his ministry to many who have not heard him in person.

Derek Prince

ONE

The Trap Door Falls

The young man was kneeling in his cell with the priest beside him. He only had a few minutes to live. Along with a dozen other people, I looked silently into the cell as I passed on my way to the open courtyard. There stood the scaffold.

As we awaited his execution, I pondered the story of this young man.

He had burst in on a sleeping couple in a small settlement south of Auckland, shot them both dead and stolen a large sum of money from their home.

Those close to him said he appeared mentally retarded. It was apparent by now, however, that the Government had to show the public its abhorrence of murder. Pleas on behalf of the young man were turned down by the Executive Council. The death penalty was his fate.

As the time for the execution drew near, I felt it would be good for me to attend, if possible, in order to see the effect on the participants.

I could recall the day when, as a young child attending primary school, they had hanged a murderer at 8 o'clock one morning. Everybody in the playground stopped at that moment. We heard subsequently that this criminal had not been properly hanged and had endured an awful death by strangulation.

Through a friend who was a Justice of the Peace, I applied to attend the hanging. To my surprise, permission was granted and I was told to report to the prison at 7pm the next day.

I had dinner at home and then told my wife I was going to a school committee meeting. I did not want her to know I was going to attend a hanging.

My friend and I presented ourselves at the prison gates promptly at 7pm. We were taken to the superintendent's office where we sat with five prison officials who were also to attend the hanging.

We watched the arm of the clock go round towards 8 o'clock. Everybody was waiting to see whether a last-minute reprieve would be granted.

At 7.55pm the superintendent said, "There is going to be no reprieve, let us go down to the scaffold."

We had been told previously that considerable precautions were taken in regard to hangings.

The scaffold was situated adjacent to the prisoner's cell. For some days previously the official in charge of the hanging, the registrar of the Supreme Court, attended daily while a sandbag was dropped through the trap door of the scaffold with the rope attached. The sandbag was the weight of the victim's body and this procedure was to ensure the rope was the correct length.

Care also had to be taken to ensure that the knot in the noose was correctly placed on the side of the victim's jaw, so that as he dropped to the end of the rope his jaw would be snapped to one side and his neck broken. In this way death would be instantaneous. If this did not happen properly, he would be strangled to death.

Knowing all of this background, we began, with trepidation, our trip towards the scaffold.

As we walked past the cells and down the various steel gangways in the prison, all was silent. We were told to walk very quietly. We had taken off our shoes because the prison officials did not want the other prisoners to know about the hanging. They were concerned there would be a riot.

Finally we came to a cell situated on the ground floor. We could see the young man seated in there with the priest, who was praying.

In an open courtyard and under the glare of the lights, we could see the scaffold with about 20 steps leading up to it and the rope with a noose hanging above the trapdoor.

A few minutes later, a procession came out of the cell. It consisted of the priest, the young man, then a warder. Slowly the man mounted the scaffold and stood on the trap door.

The registrar who was to signal the execution stood half way down the stairway. He looked up at the prisoner and asked him whether he had any last words to say.

The condemned man said, "I want to thank everybody for all they have done for me."

A black hood was then placed over the prisoner's face and the noose secured with the knot at the side of his neck.

Two hooded executioners stood on either side of the prisoner but clear of the trap door.

The registrar was standing with a sheaf of papers in his hand and without warning he raised them in the air. Obviously it was a signal to the executioners, for at that moment the trap door opened and the prisoner fell through and swung at the end of the rope. It had all happened in a flash and without sound other than the thud of the body reaching the end of the rope.

He was swinging about one metre clear of the ground.

We watched for about five minutes and then went back to the superintendent's office.

We all sat there for about an hour, drinking whisky as the shock of what we had seen began to sink in.

At the end of an hour the coroner came to view the body. We asked whether we could see it as well but permission was refused. The coroner pronounced the prisoner dead and his body was delivered to the relatives the next morning.

The important thing I learned from this experience was the effect on those participating. When he was appointed registrar of the Supreme Court, this man had not expected that he would have to take part in executions.

I knew him quite well and as he began to do more and more executions, his health failed.

Each of his successors suffered from ulcers or heart attacks as they participated.

The Government's decisions on executions continued to be inconsistent. They commuted the death sentence on some people, but allowed it to happen with others. There seemed no real pattern of justice.

When the Queen of England was visiting New Zealand in the early 1950s, a woman was due to be executed for the particularly vicious murder of three people. At the same time, four young men from Niue Island had been condemned to death and four scaffolds were transported to that island in order to carry out the execution. At the last moment, an appeal was made on their behalf to the Supreme Court of New Zealand because it was claimed they were under 16 years of age. Executions were not permitted on persons under that age.

I went to their trial in Auckland, and when I looked at them I was sure they were below 16. Because of the lack of birth certificates, nobody could really tell their age. The court finally disallowed their appeal.

However, the Government decided to commute the death sentence on the woman murderer because it was felt it would be inappropriate to hang a woman while the Queen was in New Zealand. On the other hand, they were perfectly happy to allow the four Niue Islanders to be executed because they were men.

In the ensuing outcry, the Government gave in and commuted the death sentences of the four young men to life imprisonment.

It was clear that the decisions of the Executive Council were mainly governed by political considerations. Whenever an election was approaching, the death sentence would be carried out but on other occasions it would be commuted.

About 10 years later, following a free vote in Parliament, the death penalty was finally abolished from the statute books of New Zealand.

At that time I concluded that the death sentence was inappropriate because of the inconsistency of its application.

TWO

When I Was Young

It was a lovely sunny day. I was eight years of age and playing hide and seek with my friends in an open paddock near my home when suddenly a friend of my mother's came rushing across the field shouting, "Billy, Billy, you are wanted at home."

My heart sank, knowing what it would be.

My younger brother, Keith, aged five, had been ill for about 18 months. Nobody knew what the problem was for the first few months, but then the doctors diagnosed it as cancer of the kidneys. They took him to hospital for some time, then finally sent him home to die. They said they could do no more.

While he was in hospital I boarded with friends. They were very kind but I was extremely lonely and unhappy because I had not been away from home before. I was glad when Keith came home from hospital so that at least I could go home again.

On Sunday afternoons my parents used to put him in a wheelchair and we would wheel him down Dominion Road in Auckland. There was not much traffic in those days.

It is surprising how much even a child of eight observes about his parents at times like that. I knew my father and, in particular, my mother were suffering deeply as they watched Keith become increasingly white and thin as the sickness developed and he neared death. I watched my mother grow older each day. Although still in her forties, her hair went white over a period of 18 months.

As I ran into the house that day my mother grabbed me, crying, "You are all we have now, you are all we have now." Although she had a son by an earlier marriage, he was much older and she was clearly thinking of her younger children.

They took me into the room. Keith was lying quite still. Somebody had a mirror in front of his face, checking to see whether any mist appeared on it in case he was still breathing. He wasn't.

Apparently Keith had called out in a faint voice, "Mummy, Daddy, come here quickly, come here quickly."

They rushed into the room and for a moment he sat up and colour returned to his face. His eyes were shining and he looked normal. He was looking upwards and said, "Mummy and Daddy" — there was great expectancy in his voice — "I have to go now, I have to go now. Goodbye." It was clear he had a vision of heaven, that the angels had come to take him. There was no fear, he just went.

They took Keith away. The next day they brought him back in a little white coffin. I still remember that coffin. They placed it near a window in the corner of the lounge. It was open, with a thin gauze sheet over the body. My mother never left his side for the next 24 hours.

There was a radio programme each morning especially designed for children and they used to speak out the names of various children. Once or twice they had spoken about Keith. This morning the announcer said that Keith was no longer with us and he extended condolences to the family.

The next day they buried Keith. The funeral service was held in our home and they carried the coffin out the front door into a huge hearse. I had never been in such a modern car and was quite thrilled to be sitting in the back seat.

The coffin was directly behind us with all the flowers. Our house had been full of flowers. I can still smell them.

They drove us to the cemetery with a number of cars following. On the way I saw one of my friends walking down the footpath. He looked at the hearse and I stood up and waved at him, so pleased to be in that big car. My parents pulled me back to the seat and told me not to be silly.

We came to the cemetery. It was such a big hole. They threw some dirt on the coffin and the minister said some words. Then they lowered the coffin slowly into the grave and threw some shovels full of dirt on it.

My mother didn't ever get over Keith's death. For the next 14 years he was never far from her memory. When I met my future wife, Pat, and took her home, the first thing my mother told her about was my younger brother who had died.

Every Sunday afternoon for eight years we visited his grave and placed flowers on it.

Keith's death is undoubtedly the most vivid memory of my childhood, though several other aspects of those early years also stand out.

My mother and father joined a small closed Brethren group who were very regulated and restrictive, not allowing me to play football or listen to the radio. Every Wednesday night and twice every Sunday we went to a little house church. Everybody stood up and gave testimonies about what God had done in their lives that week. Then they spoke from the Scriptures.

It was all terribly solemn and I hated it.

At 14 I told my parents I was not going back to that church again, and in the meantime I played football, listened to the radio and did all the things they said I should not be doing.

Our family was gripped by poverty, which I quickly grew to resent, determining that when I grew up I would be wealthy. This drive was fostered over many years of financial humiliation — like receiving second-hand clothes from the local council — and ultimately became an obsession.

Despite the disapproval of my parents' church, at every opportunity I went and watched sports being played. I especially loved football and cricket. Fortunately my father shared some of these interests, even though he was attending the church, so he allowed some laxity towards me in this regard.

Another luxury I enjoyed was pig-hunting with my father in many of the bush-covered areas around Auckland. By now World War II had started and petrol was rationed. We had an old Essex car which we had turned into a truck by cutting off the back section and putting a truck tray on to it. We found that it could run on kerosene, which was freely available.

We started up the truck on petrol and ran it a few miles. As soon as the carburettor was hot, we turned a switch and it would run on kerosene. In this way we were able to travel many miles to find our hunting grounds.

When I was 13 I was proud to be part of an exciting chapter in the history of Auckland and New Zealand with the establishment of the first regular air service between the United States and New Zealand.

Thousands of Aucklanders gathered at the waterfront to watch the first Pan American World Airways flying boat land. To those present, it was an immense aircraft, able to carry about 40 passengers.

As I moved amid the throng of spectators who watched the plane arrive, a well-dressed man approached me. He was a visitor to Auckland and wondered whether I could show him some of the sights. He showed me his car, which was the very latest model, and without hesitation I climbed into the vehicle and sat in the front seat alongside him.

I suggested that we go to the top of Mt Eden, which provided an excellent vista across the whole of Auckland. We then travelled via the coast to some of the eastern suburbs and came into less settled countryside. As we drove, my early eagerness and excitement turned to unease at something about the man.

When I suggested we turn around and go back to the city, he suddenly stopped the vehicle and I could see something terrible happening to him as he began to writhe around.

He managed to control himself, but a few moments later he put his hand on my private parts and suggested that I undressed. I didn't know what homosexuality was, but by then I knew I was in real trouble and I refused to do so.

The writhing started again and the man battled to control himself until, with a loud grunt, he managed to get himself under control.

I was greatly relieved when he started up the car again and we drew back towards the city. Only God knows the escape that I had that day from possible violence or even death.

THREE

The Way To Prosperity

By the time I turned 16, I had decided that the only way I could become wealthy was to be a lawyer.

I had no special ability with my hands, so could not be a carpenter. Similarly, with no bent towards mathematics, I felt I could not be an accountant. The only thing left was law.

When I told my mother she was appalled. She remembered the lawyers who tempted Jesus Christ and said, "They are a bad lot." Initially my parents forbade me to study law at university.

One of the prerequisites to studying law in those days was that you had to pass your degree in Latin. While at secondary school, I had not been very proficient at Latin and had failed in the University Entrance examinations, although I passed sufficient subjects to qualify for entrance to the university.

When I went to university to do a general arts course, the Latin professor took one look at my previous marks and told me to go and have some tuition and come back the next year.

In my first year I sat my five arts subjects and passed all of them. By now my parents were becoming proud of my efforts, so they did not strongly object to me enrolling in law the next year.

When the Latin professor saw me the following February, he asked whether I had taken tuition the previous year. I said I had not had time to do it. Having passed in five other subjects, he could not now prevent me from enrolling in law so he reluctantly accepted me as a law student.

In that first term I worked on Latin as never before and by the end of it came second in the class. Thereafter the attitude of the professor changed totally and in my subsequent years at university he always adopted a kindly attitude towards me.

By the time I had passed my first year's exams I felt well on the way to becoming a lawyer.

In my second year at university, I began to work in the Public Trust Office, which administered estates of deceased people as well as trusts. However, the working atmosphere was stifling and a hindrance to my studies, so at the end of a few months I gave up the job.

The war was still on and I had to have a job in an essential industry so I was "manpowered" into the Westfield Freezing Works. Here I found myself doing shift work at all hours of the day and night among some of the most hardened individuals I have met.

I had to work in cool rooms adjacent to killing chains. The animals were frozen and we loaded the carcasses into various freezing departments. Then they were loaded into railway wagons next to the works for export.

On each of the floors of the freezing chambers there was a circular trap door, through which you could look down several floors.

The men among whom I was working were involved in

various perverted practices. One day one of them stood with a knife at my back and said that if I did not agree to having sex with him, he would throw me down the hatch. Fortunately, some of my workmates came into the freezing department at that moment and I escaped.

Although the hours of work were very onerous, I was earning good money. Often our shifts would start at 1am and last till 6am, or from 4pm until midnight.

I had turned my back on Christianity, and at university read every book I could on agnosticism and atheism.

I also became immersed in politics, joined the local branch of the Labour Party, and at 19 was president of that branch and organiser for a political candidate. Politics became my escape route from God. Political involvement eased my conscience and convinced me I was doing my bit for the community.

I had a hunger to become involved politically and looked forward to the age of 21 when I could stand for Parliament. With this in mind, I was glad when one of my friends, Warren Freer, who was quite a lot older than me, was nominated to stand for Parliament and asked me to join him on the platform. Standing on the soap boxes around the Eden electorate with Warren, I would speak first and then he would speak. He missed out on that seat, but subsequently was elected to an adjacent seat and went on to become a Minister of the Crown in the third Labour Government.

My work, university and political involvement left little time for the pleasures of life. But as the war neared an end, I took up dancing lessons and frequently attended dances around Auckland. In those days they were very respectable affairs and it was the practice of the young man to ask a girl, who was seated, for a dance.

At the age of 19, I attended a dance in one of the local halls and as I looked around, I saw a young lady with beautiful hair. Women's hair had always been attractive to me, but this particular person had light brown hair flecked with blonde that reached down to her shoulders. It was gorgeous and I approached her and asked her to dance. She was a most proficient dancer, so we had several dances and I asked whether I could take her home that night. She agreed, and a short while later we went to a ball together.

When I asked her out again the following Sunday, I was astounded when she said she could not come because she was an Anglican and taught at Sunday school. I was a professing atheist and I found, to my dismay, that I was falling in love with somebody who called herself a Christian.

Pat and I went out together for the next two and a half years. When my mother found out about her, and especially her Christian background, it encouraged her to pray even harder for her rebellious son. I didn't realise it then, but for 10 years she had prayed for me daily.

By the time I was 21, I had completed my university studies and my parents were very proud as they watched me take the oaths to be admitted as a barrister and solicitor of the Supreme Court of New Zealand.

During the last two years of my law course, I had worked in a legal office, receiving a sum equivalent to $3 per week. The first four days of the week I worked in the office learning practical law and on the Friday dug my employer's garden. This was part of the contract with him.

As the time approached for the completion of my law course and my admission as a barrister and solicitor, I looked for an office where I could set up in practice. I had nothing to lose as I was earning virtually nothing anyway.

I found premises where I could work by arrangement with another legal firm, who agreed to give me some work. After I was admitted to the Bar, my sign was put up outside my new office, "W.A. Subritzky, Barrister and Solicitor". I was on my way to making my fortune.

By now I had given up the idea of a full-time political career, and declined an opportunity of standing as a candidate for the Labour Party in favour of going on with law.

I well remember my first client. I had placed a notice in the newspaper announcing my new business and this man travelled about 50 kilometres to see me, arriving the day after I opened my office.

I felt certain I could handle any problem, but this man stumped me with his first question. He said that he and his wife had been separated for some months and she was now committing adultery. He wanted to know if he could procure a divorce immediately.

I racked my brain, but could not think of the answer to his question. However, I said to him, "Last week I noticed in the law reports that there was a decision affecting the very situation which you have raised. If you will give me a couple of days to look up the case, I am sure I can give you the best answer you can get."

In fact, there had been no such case, but I was now given the opportunity to look up the answer to his question. Two days later, he came in again and by now I had fully acquainted myself with the correct legal position and was able to give him his answer.

My main source of clients in those early days was people I already knew.

During the previous three years I had joined football committees, school committees, old people's committees and young people's committees. I joined every committee that would have me. In those days you could not advertise that you were practising as a lawyer so you had to get your clients by recommendation. Committees served this purpose nicely.

At 19 I was elected to the committee of the school which I had left at 13. Technically it was not possible for me to be elected before I was 21, but I found a way around it by renting a room in my parents' home and therefore became a householder and eligible for election.

FOUR

Getting My Own Way

My relationship with Pat became deeper and more intense as the months went by.

We often talked about the future, and had decided in principle that we would marry one day. And yet two years after we began going out, I still hadn't taken her home to meet my parents!

Then Pat told me quite bluntly that if we did not get married by the next Christmas I could forget it.

We were engaged in August and I went home and told my mother and father. Mum was deeply shocked, but when I brought Pat home, she immediately liked her and during the next few months they became firm friends.

There was still one obstacle, however.

Pat wanted to get married in the Anglican Church and the vicar would not marry us because I was not a Christian. He told me, however, that if I would come to his home for an hour each Saturday morning for eight weeks for instruction in the Christian faith, he would marry us. I agreed to do so.

I was faithful to my promise, but each session ended in an argument. I knew quite a lot about the Bible because I had read it in my early teenage years at my parents' church, and I had no time for people who were ordained as ministers and wore clerical clothes. So each Saturday, I would ask the vicar many questions, and finally he would throw up his hands and say, "Go and see the bishop. I do not have the answer to your question."

I did not want to see any bishop. I just wanted to get married. So the following Saturday I would attend his study again. At the end of eight weeks he gave up and agreed to marry us, which he duly did on December 18, 1948.

By now my mother was quite ill, though she was able to attend the wedding ceremony. However, she died after an operation the following April, still praying for her errant son.

I was called upon to make the funeral arrangements. My mother was to be buried in the same grave as young Keith had been buried in 14 years before. When the undertaker and I arrived at the cemetery to inspect the grave, it had been opened. The sexton told us that he had dug the grave as deep as he could without touching the coffin that was already there. However, one of the workmen lifted up a plank and dropped one end into the grave. It hit one end of Keith's coffin which jumped in the air about one metre and fell back. Shocked and sickened, I walked away from the cemetery.

After our marriage we had moved in with my parents as there was no other accommodation available. So when my mother passed away, we looked forward to comforting my father, who had been a devoted husband.

However, about two weeks after her death he changed abruptly. He began going out constantly at night and it was apparent that he was seeing another woman.

About a month later he announced that he was going to marry this woman, who had been married three times before. We could see it was a mistake but he was obsessed with her. Despite our pleas, my father married her and demanded that we purchase the home from him or he would evict us. He was a changed person, no longer the father I knew.

One day Pat and I came home to find that the whole house had been stripped, including our own belongings. He had taken them away to an auction and sold them.

Shortly afterwards we entered into a contract with my father to buy the house and that was the last we saw of him for some time.

While we settled into married life reasonably happily, there was one area in which we were poles apart — faith in God.

Pat continued to attend the local Anglican church each Sunday morning, but I refused to go with her. I stubbornly refused to acknowledge God, or to have anything to do with church.

However, about six months after we were married, Pat turned to me as she was preparing to go to church and said, "Why don't you come along after the service because they are going to elect a committee for the church?" She emphasised the word "after".

When she had gone, I pondered the situation. Here was an opportunity to join another committee, a matter dear to my heart. By now my practice was flourishing as more and more people were coming to see me, many of them because of my involvement in committees.

I did not have long to make up my mind because the Anglican services usually last only one hour. After about 30 minutes I determined to go to the meeting and quickly showered and dressed. At 11am I presented myself at the hall behind the church and within a few minutes was elected to the vestry, although I had never heard the term "vestry" before.

I was elected because I was well known to several people in the meeting. I already served on the local school committee and various other committees. These people felt it would be good for me to be on the church vestry.

After the meeting, the vicar, a very large man called Canon Small, came to me. "Welcome young man, glad to see you here at the meeting," he said. "I will see you next Sunday in church."

"No, I don't intend to come to church," I told him. He looked somewhat surprised and said, "Well if you don't come to church you can't be on the vestry."

I went away and thought about the situation. As a lawyer I looked up the rules governing attendance at the Anglican Church. There I found that Anglicans were expected to take communion at least twice a year, at Christmas and Easter. I felt I could do this.

At the next vestry meeting, the vicar asked what I proposed to do about church and I told him, "You will see me at Christmas and Easter." He was a very wise man and said nothing.

Despite this resolution, I gradually began to go to church more often. They spoke about church in the vestry meetings and it made me curious about what went on there. I was familiar with the communion service because these had been held in the church I had attended as a child. Accordingly, when people went forward to the rail for communion, I went with them.

The years went by, and I began attending church regularly. The Bible was still a mystery to me. Many times I tried to read it but I could not make sense of it. Other times I tried to pray but I seemed to strike a brick wall.

As time passed, I was elected to further committees in the church. Soon I was on the governing body of the local diocese named the synod, which governed about 80 parishes. Then I was elected to the stewardship council and became chairman of it. This council was responsible for ensuring sufficient funds were raised to support the whole diocese. This meant I had to travel to many parishes with the bishop and often I spoke in the meetings to encourage people to give to the church.

A new hunger was developing within me. I did not understand it, but felt something was missing in my life.

For the next 20 years I served on the church synod and on the vestry without having any personal knowledge of Jesus Christ as my personal Saviour.

FIVE

From Rags to Riches

The desire to be wealthy had never left me, and I quickly realised that to make money in any quantity I had to get other people working for me.

Therefore, after just a year as a barrister and solicitor, I had my first attempt at business.

In those days New Zealand was subject to heavy import licensing, so if anyone was fortunate enough to start the right type of business, they had government protection from imports as well as special taxation benefits.

I was constantly being approached by clients to go into partnership in various business ventures and finally I succumbed to a proposal from a friend to enter a cardboard box-making business. We rented a small building not far from my home and purchased the necessary equipment. I borrowed heavily for this purpose.

My friend was also keen on printing so we purchased a large amount of printing equipment and acquired the local suburban newspaper.

Before long we were employing about 15 staff, but it seemed no matter how much we printed or how much work we did, we could not achieve a profit.

As for the box-making, we were producing tens of thousands of cardboard boxes for industrial purposes but still were not successful financially.

After about nine months I decided we should close down the business because it would have taken all my time to turn it around. I could not afford to do this. My partner was angry, but I still felt it was the right thing to do. We sold the equipment at a loss and thus my first business venture ended in failure.

About a year later, I was approached by a relative to assist him with a major problem. He had served overseas for four years during the war and had come home and started a building business, acquiring a nice home with a heavy mortgage.

Later, as a result of his war service, he became very ill and the person to whom he owed the money called up the mortgage on his home.

It looked as though the house would have to be sold, although I tried every method to save the situation. Finally it seemed that the only way was to attempt to have the mortgage document declared invalid. This was largely a bluff on my part, but I wrote to the lawyer concerned to say we would be challenging the mortgage document in court and holding him responsible in damages for the action he was taking. This scared the lawyer because not only was he suing on behalf of his client, but he was the one who had drawn up the mortgage.

Shortly afterwards he and his client agreed to give my relative an extension. He soon recovered from his illness and brought his arrears up to date and the problem was solved.

Some time later the same client introduced me to a man of Jewish extraction who had recently come from Europe. The man, Richard, told me he had visited many of the islands in the Pacific where the war had been fought and had acquired the rights to much of the surplus war equipment the Americans had left behind. He was shipping this equipment to Australia and other countries and making a fortune from it. He was specialising in engines which had never been used and air-strip matting which had covered many of the temporary airfields constructed during the war.

Richard told me he needed a partner. He said he was required to travel widely, but felt that if somebody like me would join him in partnership, we could have a very profitable business.

As he expanded on the facts and figures, I became greedy, seeing the chance of becoming extremely wealthy.

We set up an office in the same building as my law practice and appointed a manager.

Richard told me that if we could acquire a ship rather than chartering one, as he had in the past, the whole operation would be more flexible and would make more money.

We looked around for a suitable vessel and finally purchased one from the Holm Shipping Company which had been used between New Zealand and the Chatham Islands, about 1120 kilometres east of New Zealand. It was a 300-tonne vessel with a crew of 22.

We took over the vessel in Auckland, and soon it was sailing to Sydney, Australia, with a full cargo.

To mark its departure and the beginning of the shipping company, Richard invited Pat and me to dinner at his home. His wife was a beautiful lady who was a marvellous cook. We had an 11-course meal which was wonderfully presented. It was not until afterwards that I discovered I had eaten snails! Richard and I then prepared to go to Australia to meet the vessel. In those days the only air transport was by flying boat which took about nine hours. Richard went over first and about two weeks later I went to join him. In the meantime I had arranged another friend to take care of my legal practice.

When I arrived in Sydney, Richard was waiting for me, and to my surprise he introduced me to a young lady with whom he was obviously on very close terms.

The ship had already arrived, but my partner had dismissed the skipper, whom he said was incompetent. The new captain was preparing to sail to the New Hebrides (now called Vanuatu), a journey of about 10 days.

In the meantime, we flew to New Caledonia as I brushed up on my schoolboy French so I could deal with the various French companies there.

We proposed to send to New Caledonia and the New Hebrides mainly tinned meat and beer. Canned food was particularly popular in those days.

The ship left Sydney with a full cargo headed for the New Hebrides. It was my job to arrange a major dinner and invite the British and French High Commissioners, together with the governor and other high officials. This dinner, at Port Vila, was to mark the opening of the first regular shipping service to the New Hebrides.

My trip to the New Hebrides was a lengthy one by flying boat. There was a weekly service and I noticed as we landed on Port Vila Harbour that there was the wreckage of a flying boat piled up against the shore. About six months earlier, it had hit a reef and crashed as it landed.

I had fixed the date for the dinner function and waited for the vessel to arrive. It should have taken about 10 days to reach the New Hebrides but at the end of that time there was no sign of it. We kept in daily contact but the skipper seemed unclear as to his position.

He and the first mate had previously been the officers in charge of a 10,000-tonne vessel, and we were unaware that neither of them had done navigation for many years. Nor were we aware that they had taken many cases of gin on board for their personal use during the trip.

Day after day went by. Still no sign of the vessel. We were receiving regular radio messages but by now it was clear that they did not know where they were. Soon we received a message that they were running out of water.

I was keeping Richard in Sydney acquainted with the situation and he kept pressing me to try and find the vessel. He also warned me not to let any other vessel place a tow-rope on the ship if it was found or even let people land on it, because they would immediately make a salvage claim.

Another week went by. The dinner was postponed and I was becoming a laughing stock in Vila.

Finally, in desperation, I contacted the commander of the Royal New Zealand Air Force in Suva, Fiji, which had a small fleet of float planes. He agreed to come and search for the vessel and for several days the planes went out from Port Vila — but they, too, were unsuccessful.

When the squadron leader came to me and said they could not go out any more, I produced a case of whisky and he agreed to go out for another day.

To my great relief, on that day they found the vessel. They put it on course for the New Hebrides and then flew back to Suva. I was very grateful for their help.

Finally, the vessel approached Port Vila Harbour. I sent

out a pilot who brought it into the wharf. I had arranged for many workers to unload the vessel, even through the afternoon siesta, because we wanted to get it away to Santos, another island in the New Hebrides group.

The day after its arrival, Richard flew in from Sydney with a new skipper and first mate.

His plane arrived over Port Vila just as another nightmarish episode was occurring with the ship.

After it had unloaded its cargo for Port Vila, the ship left at 6pm that night for Santos.

Early the next morning I received a message that it was returning to harbour because the captain found a stowaway on board.

I rushed to the radio station, which was on an adjacent hill, and watched the vessel approach the harbour. When it had come in previously, the tide had been full and the vessel had a pilot. Now the vessel was approaching the harbour at low tide and with no pilot.

I ran on to the end of the wharf and waved to the skipper with all my might as the vessel approached, trying to get it to stop. I knew it could hit a sandbank.

I saw the skipper looking at me and heard him sound the ship's bells. Then he sounded full ahead. He obviously was not going to take any notice of me. A few minutes later there was a terrific crash as the vessel struck a sandbank, leaving it stuck in the middle of the harbour on a direct line to where the flying boat should land.

I returned to the radio station and heard the pilot of the plane blaspheming all and sundry, and particularly the skipper. The pilot was saying his landing would now be extremely hazardous as the ship was in the way. Finally he did land the plane successfully.

When my partner stepped off the plane he was in a violent mood. He had a stack of newspapers in his hand, and said I had made a fool of him and the company.

While waiting for the vessel, I had cabled Pat in New Zealand to come to Vila as I could see I would be there for some time. While she was in Sydney on her way to Vila, I contacted her to say that the vessel was missing. She told the agent, who in turn told the newspapers. Exaggerated stories began to appear of how the vessel had left Sydney without proper survey. The papers were full of the story as day by day we could not find the vessel. Richard had been helpless to prevent this publicity, while I had been unaware of it.

Richard did not have a very good grasp of English. When I had cabled him to say the vessel was running out of water, he thought I had meant that it was out of the water or that it had hit a reef. He demanded to know why I had not left the vessel on the reef so we could have claimed the insurance!

Richard promptly replaced the captain and first mate on the vessel and we went ahead with our inaugural dinner. The shipping service seemed to be under way.

I flew up to Santos and ensured the ship was properly laden. While there, I was wandering through the jungle adjacent to one of the old air strips and came across an enormous propeller. It had come from one of the United States aircraft carriers. As we had the rights to both the airfield and everything around it, I promptly arranged for the propeller to be shipped back to Australia.

About this time, the French authorities in Noumea put on public tender much more material which had been left by the Americans in Santos.

After the war, the Americans had offered the water system in Port Vila to the British and French authorities. They had laid a complete water system through the town. However, the British and French authorities refused to pay for it, believing the Americans could do nothing about it. Instead, the Americans dragged all the pipes out of the ground and dumped the whole system in the sea.

In an effort to prevent war supplies being given away, the Americans bulldozed many trucks and other vehicles into the harbour near Santos. The area became known as Million Dollar Point.

Now the French authorities were putting this point up to tender because of the value of the scrap metal buried in the area.

Richard and I tendered for the right to extract the scrap, and we knew our tender was the highest. But the authorities gave the contract to a lower tenderer whom they favoured.

Richard then hired a barge with a crane on it and began to extract the materials with a crane from the barge situated on the water. The authorities could do nothing about it. Eventually they gave in and we were awarded the contract.

We found many surplus materials, including GM engines still in their original wrappings. All of these were loaded on board and the ship made its return journey to Australia.

I returned to Sydney, and made it my base for the next few months. On a number of occasions I flew back to New Zealand, a long journey in the old flying boats. On one occasion they put the wrong oil in the engines and the plane began to fail about 500 kilometres east of Sydney as we crossed the Tasman Sea. We returned to Sydney, flying only a few metres above the water and barely made it.

Although the vessel was doing various trips to Vanuatu, our bank balance was running low. The cost of running the vessel was enormous and we did not seem to be making much headway financially.

Through various channels, I found that Richard had a considerable sum of money in his bank account, so I cabled him in Europe, where he had gone with his lady friend, and told him that he must either return immediately or give me access to this money. He was amazed that I had heard about it but he eventually gave permission for me to use some of the money.

However, this money was soon gone as well.

On the next voyage from the New Hebrides, the ship brought a full cargo of GM motors.

I had no idea of their worth, and was desperate for money, so when the vessel arrived in Sydney, I arranged for an auction to sell these motors. As they were unloaded from the vessel by the hundreds, they were auctioned for as low as $20 each. However, I got the money needed to keep the venture afloat.

When Richard returned to Sydney, he was beside himself when he ascertained the price at which I had sold the motors. They had, in fact, been worth many hundreds of dollars each.

Another financial crisis arose, again while Richard was overseas, when my bank manager in New Zealand informed me that the bank would give us no further financial assistance.

I decided on radical measures. I told him I would pay his plane fare from Auckland to Melbourne, Australia, and asked to meet his top officials. The plan worked. The head office of the bank was so impressed that it agreed to further funding.

This lasted for some time, until Richard returned to Sydney and agreed to purchase my share of the business.

I took a mortgage over the ship to cover the value of what he owed me and returned to New Zealand and my law practice.

About two months later the first payment fell due, but there was no sign of the money. I knew Richard could afford to pay me but was trying to avoid doing so. Eventually, Richard offered me a small part of the instalment, but I refused to accept it and instead instructed solicitors in Sydney to arrest the vessel by placing a writ on its mast.

The solicitors were very reluctant to do this as it had been 50 years since a vessel had been arrested in Sydney and they were unsure of the consequences. They pointed out that if I was not entitled to place the writ there, both of us would be liable in damages. However, I was able to satisfy them that the money was owing to me so the writ was placed on the mast.

Richard went berserk, saying his credibility had been destroyed. However, I felt that he had no intention of paying me and that my action was justified.

Gradually he offered more and more of the instalment due. I refused to remove the writ. The solicitors were anxious. Finally he agreed to pay the total instalment and the writ was removed.

I knew this would not be the end of the matter, and suspected I might receive an attack on my integrity.

I therefore went to the chairman of the Ethics Committee of the Law Society in Auckland and explained my circumstances to him. I told him that if I had done anything wrong ethically he should tell me and I would amend it. He assured me I had not. I then told him that I wanted him to be my lawyer in the event of any problem.

I also instructed another lawyer, who was far less gentlemanly than the first man. Richard could resort to very dirty tactics, so I wanted a lawyer capable of handling him.

This did not take long. Shortly afterwards Richard arrived in New Zealand by flying boat. It landed on the Auckland Harbour and you could almost hear him yelling as he got off the plane. He immediately instructed another top lawyer in the city, giving his version of the facts.

In the meantime, however, I had taken another step. I knew Richard owed a substantial sum to another friend of mine so he would be reluctant to meet him. I arranged with this friend that I should sell for a nominal sum the debt owing to me by my partner, pointing out that in this way my partner would have to confront him.

Shortly after my partner's arrival, his lawyer telephoned me. "Subritzky, I want to talk to you about the money which is owed to you." I said no money was owing to me.

"Don't be a fool, Subritzky, you know money is owing to you."

"No," I replied. "I have sold that debt." I named this party. There was silence at the end of the phone as the lawyer told my partner of the transaction.

The lawyer came back on the phone. He wanted to meet with me. I said, "No, you will have to meet with my lawyers." Again there was a stunned silence.

I then told him the name of my lawyers and he recognised one as the chairman of the Ethics Committee and the other as a very capable criminal lawyer.

Finally he gave up.

Richard did not go and see the man to whom he owed money, but instead returned to Australia. I promptly purchased the debt back from my friend, so now I held the mortgage again.

One month later the next instalment fell due. The ship was again in Sydney. I demanded payment. A partial offer was again forthcoming. I refused it and demanded that the ship be arrested. Again a writ was placed on the mast and the same performance occurred, with the Sydney solicitors being approached by Richard's solicitors offering various sums of money. I refused to accept them and instead received the full instalment.

Once again, Richard came hurriedly by plane to New Zealand. In the meantime, I sold the debt back to my friend.

The same performance occurred. Richard's lawyer called me to discuss the matter. I referred him to my lawyers and told him also that my former partner owed me no money as I had transferred the debt. Again there was a stunned silence.

Richard returned to Australia and in due course the third instalment fell due. In the meantime I had purchased the debt back and enforced it again by writ. Again the same performance occurred, with Richard returning to New Zealand after paying that instalment. Again the lawyer called me and again I told him I no longer held the debt and also referred him to my lawyers. This time, Richard returned to Australia and gave up, after which I began to receive the instalments regularly.

Some years later, Richard's lawyer became a judge. Once I met him at a function and he immediately reminded me of the whole episode. He told me that he found my former partner a real problem to deal with.

I thought the episode had ended as I didn't hear or see anything from my former partner for many years.

But about 25 years later, as I was sitting in my legal office, my secretary came to me and told me that a man named Richard was waiting to see me.

He was very jovial and we sat and chatted for a little while.

"Well, Beel (as he called me), you were extremely clever before. I admire you for it," he said.

Then he told me that he owned a large tract of land in Queensland which would be a marvellous investment.

Needless to say, I was not interested, but marvelled at the thickness of his skin.

Thus, my second business venture also ended unsatisfactorily, though my drive to succeed and make money was unabated.

I had continued my law firm throughout the ups and downs of the other business escapades, and it was through this avenue that my dreams of fortune began to become a reality.

About six months after I first set up the law practice, I realised my offices were unsuitable. However, in those days office space was very hard to find and shifting was going to be no easy task.

One day, following newspaper advertisements, I received a rather mysterious call from a bank manager whose offices were on a secondary street, away from the centre of Auckland. He said he could offer me some offices, but I told him I wasn't interested as I wanted to stay in the main street.

However, he was persistent, saying he would give me some of the bank's legal business. The offer was very tempting, and a few months later we moved into these premises above the bank and began receiving a lot of the bank's business.

In those days it was difficult for people to obtain second mortgage finance, but it was necessary for most people to get a second mortgage to buy a home. Eventually I persuaded the bank to begin lending on second mortgages and in this way introduced it to hundreds of new clients each year. I told the bank I would do my utmost to ensure that its clients complied with the mortgages. None of these people failed me. Such advances meant my practice began to widen immensely. Soon I was servicing nearly 1000 clients at a time and was working up to 80 hours a week. Before long I was working six and even seven days a week, and many long hours at night.

I soon decided that criminal work was not for me because of the time spent around the courts waiting for cases to be heard. I found that I could make much more money handling conveyancing transactions.

However, as time went by, I realised again that all the money I was making was from my own efforts and that I would never get really wealthy because of the limitations of my own personal time.

Therefore I again began looking elsewhere for the possibility of making money.

I had come out of the shipping venture quite well, having recovered the money I had put into it plus a reasonable profit.

I no longer wanted to be involved with ships because they floated around the sea and one never knew what was going to happen next and so I decided buying land was the best answer.

Land was a great investment in those days, and I knew our district was going to become very prosperous. I began to purchase industrial land and before long it had quadrupled in value. I went into partnership with the local land agent and between us we acquired large blocks suitable for residential development. We began to develop these into household sites, which we sold to builders.

One of these builders had developed a very large new home business and had rapidly become a millionaire. We got to know each other quite well and one Christmas, as we sat together and talked, he began to tell me about the money he was making as a builder. I pricked up my ears, realising that there was obviously much more money in home building than in land developing.

Shortly thereafter, another builder approached me with a proposition that we go into house building together. I agreed and in 1959 my housing company commenced business.

Soon my builder partner and I were acquiring land in various areas and building many homes. Between my law practice and my ventures into land and now house building, I began to achieve my main objective to make my first million dollars. I was still a young man and felt I was on the pathway to success.

Shortly afterwards, another building company approached me, and soon our combined operations were building several hundred homes a year. The arrangement with the other building company lasted three years before I sold out my interest while retaining my stakes in my own company, which went on to build many thousands of houses all around Auckland.

In order to develop our land into sections, many skills

were required. I am sure that if I had not been a lawyer, I would have been a road builder. I just loved to build roads.

When deciding whether a piece of land was suitable for subdivision, I could picture in my mind how the land would look after development.

Rather than employ a general contractor to develop the land, we would act as the contractors ourselves. We would hire all the necessary subcontractors and sub-trades and during the summer I would often spend weeks on subdivisions supervising the construction work. All the works were completed under the supervision of our engineers, but much of my time was spent organising the subcontractors on the job. I loved to be out in the open air during the summer months.

One day, 10 years after commencing house building, I was at a hot pool near Auckland. By now my company had become the main rival of the builder who had first sparked my interest in house building. As I swam, he came into the same pool, glared at me for a moment and said, "I wish you would drop dead." I was quite shocked at the remark and realised my building operations were affecting him. A few months later he himself had a heart attack.

But the rancour in our relationship lifted when we realised building firms specialising in our type of market should have an organisation to make combined representations to the Government regarding housing finance.

As we realised that there was much to be gained by co-operation, we became very friendly. Over the next few months he frequently telephoned me at night and our friendship grew. Finally he called me at 1 o'clock one morning and said, "Bill, I want to thank you for all you have done." By now the building industry grouping we had founded had become very powerful and he recognised its value.

A few days later he died unexpectedly at 47 years of age.

As I attended his funeral, I began to realise that money was not everything and that one day, like my brother Keith, and my mother, I, too, would have to die.

SIX

Money Doesn't Buy Happiness

As the years sped by, Pat and I had four children — Janne, Paul, Maria and John.

I was a poor father, however, as my commitments on the business front didn't leave much time to concentrate on home life. I never wanted to hold any of the babies, and as they grew older was incapable of showing them real love. I did my best, but I could never tell them I loved them.

I thank God now that we were given four healthy children. They were certainly a gift from God Himself, but at that time I did not appreciate the fact. I thought having children was our natural right.

In those days it was not usual for the husband to be with the wife at the time of birth. Each time Pat went into labour, I remained at home, waiting fearfully for the doctor to ring me. It was always a great relief when he finally rang to say all was well.

About eight years after we married, I decided it would be good to own a beach home, although I really did not have the money to purchase one. I visited some of the most desirable beaches and eventually came across a very valuable property on a beach front north of Auckland. As soon as Pat and I visited it, we knew we wanted it.

The day we first inspected the property, the neighbour leaned over the fence and asked whether I was interested in buying it. When I said I was, he replied, "This is the best thing you will ever do."

Subsequently we became firm friends. He was also a businessman in Auckland.

As I did so often in my career, I paid a deposit, mortgaged myself and went ahead with the purchase. I paid $30,000, and 20 years later was offered $1 million for it. It seemed that whatever I turned my hand to in the way of property multiplied in value.

For the next 20 years, we spent our Christmas holidays at our beach home. Our neighbour, Bill, was always very friendly and we enjoyed many big parties at his house.

Shortly after purchasing the beach home, I felt it necessary to buy a boat and after much shopping around, purchased a very fast eight metre vessel powered by large engines. I motored it from Auckland around to the beach home and Pat and I went out to test it out. I soon had it up and planing, its bow high in the air.

Seeing me out on the water, one of my neighbours asked whether he could do some water-skiing behind it. Wanting to show off my new boat, I agreed. Soon he was water-skiing down the bay, but as I approached the beach I did not have proper vision. The next thing I knew, Pat, sitting near the bow, was screaming loudly. We were approaching a dinghy with two people in it. I did not have time to stop, but sliced through the middle of it, throwing them into the water. It was fortunate that they were not killed.

The occupants of the boat were very reasonable, accepting a replacement of their watches and letting the incident go. However, I was rapidly learning the need for safety in boats.

Bill also had a boat and we were both keen fishermen, always trying to outdo one another. In those days fish were plentiful and I would rarely come home with fewer than 50 in my boat.

On one occasion I came up the beach to find that Bill had caught over 150 fish. As I emptied the barrels from my boat on to the beach, I found I had 170 fish.

Pat and I both loved the outdoors and we spent many wonderful summers at our beach house.

We also took up snow skiing and quickly became quite proficient. We had many friends who were ski instructors from the United States and at times we loaned them our beach home. The fact that they were not married did not concern us, nor that they were having sex. One Friday night, as we entered the beach home, Paul went directly into his bedroom, but before he could switch on the light he let out a great scream and began to weep violently. He was nine years old at the time. He ran out of the house and Pat and I rushed after him, but it was nearly an hour before we found him. When we did so, we found we had a completely different son. He had become completely rebellious.

The following year the school headmaster called me to his office and asked what was wrong with Paul. He seemed so different from his sisters. At 11 years of age, Paul asked me if he was adopted. At 12, Pat said, "If you keep him out of jail till he is 20 I'll give you a medal."

I worked hard at keeping Paul out of jail.

When he sat his School Certificate examination at the age of 14, I took six weeks off work to help him with his schooling and to ensure he succeeded. I was going to have no failures in my family.

When he was 16, he sat his University Entrance examination and again I took time off work to coach him and ensure he passed. Throughout these years, however, there was a huge gap in our relationship. One day, when he was 16, we had an argument in our lounge and he hit me on the jaw and knocked me to the floor. When I got up it felt as if I had had every tooth knocked out of my head.

I felt he needed more discipline. In New Zealand there is an organisation called Outward Bound which takes young men and trains them on a para-military basis. I enrolled Paul in one of these courses. Each morning he was woken at 5am and had to take a swim in freezing water. During the day, he and the other young men were taken for bush walks over steep country. In addition, they had to climb mountains, do rock climbing, canoeing and many other activities to ensure their discipline.

In the six weeks he was away, Paul wrote only one short letter to his mother.

On his return, I met him at the railway station. As he stepped off the train I could see he had lost a lot of weight, but when he opened his mouth he was no different. He was still mean — and now he was lean as well.

My attempts to discipline and sort him out had been a failure.

As if that wasn't enough, we also had other family problems to deal with.

One of these involved my half brother, Jack, who developed cancer. He had been a heavy smoker and now he had got melanoma.

I flew him to the United States to a friend who owned a

health farm and Jack spent six months there with his wife. When I visited him at the end of six months it was clear that he was not improving and that he would have to return home.

The owner of the health ranch flew with us to Hawaii. As we said goodbye it was clear that this would be the last time Jack would see this man and the parting was very traumatic. By now Jack was very sick and had to be lifted in a wheelchair in and out of the plane.

At one point I made some silly comment to him such as, "Oh well, when we die it is not really too different."

He turned to me and said, "If you were in my position you would not say that."

Following our mother's death years before, Jack had gone to the same church in which I had been brought up. He had attended there for several years and had also become very exclusive in his religious views. However, after about six years, he left the church.

Now, about 12 years later, he was dying of cancer.

I saw that the Bible was always beside his bed, and that he read it frequently. Month by month he was slipping back, becoming little more than skin and bone. On one occasion when I visited him he literally lifted out of the bed and began to spin as terrible pain racked his body. It was horrible to watch him dying.

One night, when Pat and I were at a party in a nightclub with some friends, I received a telephone call to go to the hospital urgently. I rushed there and arrived just in time to watch him die. One minute he was writhing in pain and the next minute a peace fell on him. I watched him breathe his last, and will never forget the gentleness with which the nurse stroked his head after he had passed away.

During his sickness Jack had made various comments

about the fact that the Bible could be understood only by those who had spiritual understanding. While this remark intrigued me, and worried me somewhat, I did not follow it up. I was just too busy.

Pat and I had every material thing we could have possibly wanted.

We had a lovely home in spacious grounds, the beach home, a boat, a new Rolls Royce.....

It had been hard work, but my drive to be wealthy had literally paid off.

However, as the old saying goes, money doesn't buy happiness. Neither can it provide a marriage that survives, or children of whom a father can be proud.

I knew our marriage was growing cold. There was a distance developing between us, and other fields began to look greener.

I had always been a loner, and it had been difficult for me to completely give myself in marriage. There was always an indescribable barrier between Pat and me, and as time went by this barrier grew.

After 20 years together, it was clear our marriage could end. Many of our friends were obtaining divorces, and it looked as though ours was on the way.

Sometimes I pondered as I drove home that if there was a God then perhaps by going to church I had some chance of getting into heaven. But if there was no God, then all of it had been a waste of time.

Sometimes, too, I thought I could end it all by driving into a car coming the other way, but I could not understand why I was getting these crazy thoughts.

Despite the turmoil, I continued travelling around the parishes with our bishop and participating in many fundraising campaigns. One day, as we were travelling in the car, the bishop asked me what I thought of admitting divorced people to communion and also of divorce and abortion as a general issue. At that time, this matter was under consideration by the church.

I really had no answer for him because I had very little idea of what the Bible said on these topics. However, I did tell him I did not see anything wrong with abortion.

Three weeks later, in his address to the synod of the church, the bishop touched on the questions of divorce and abortion. He turned and looked directly at me as he said to the whole synod, "I believe that abortion is murder." I never forgot that statement.

By now Paul was studying law in Dunedin, about 1200 kilometres from Auckland.

We were pleased he wanted to do something positive, but I was taken aback when he told me the reason he wanted to go to Dunedin rather than study in Auckland was so he could be as far away from me as possible!

His sister, Janne, was also in Dunedin studying to be a dietitian.

The first year Paul was away was not so bad, but the next year proved chaotic.

We were frequently getting calls from Janne to tell us that something had gone wrong. Usually the calls were on a Sunday morning, and she would first pacify us by saying Paul was still alive, but that he had had an accident. We never knew when we would hear from Janne to the effect that he had been killed.

Eventually I used to say, "God, if there is a God, take this boy. Don't leave him a paraplegic."

There was a certain desperation coming into my life as

our marriage was drifting apart and our home was falling apart.

SEVEN

Into the Light

Because I was only paying lip service to God — and I knew it — I was very uncomfortable when I came across churchgoers who were truly born again.

My half-brother, Jack, was one.

Another, in a completely different setting, was well-known American evangelist Billy Graham. When Billy Graham visited New Zealand, I went to hear him at Carlaw Park. A great crowd was present and as I listened to the hymns, my heart was stirred within me.

When Dr Graham made the appeal, however, I did not go forward.

I felt I did not need to as I was attending church regularly and was on my vestry, the stewardship council and many other committees. I felt that if I did go forward, my friends would laugh at me.

However, I did obtain copies of the records of some of the hymns that had been sung and played them many times.

Another challenge to my lifeless religiosity came from a man I hardly knew who was from a church of which I was highly suspicious.

I was chairman of a combined meeting of all the churches in our district and we used to meet once a month to discuss mutual projects. There were about 25 different churches involved.

Each month, as the discussion took place, I noticed that this man had very little to say, but when he did speak he was worth listening to. I began to gain considerable respect for him. He was from the Assembly of God church.

One night, following a committee meeting, he waited while the other people left my home. As he said goodbye at the front door he suddenly said to me, "Bill, unless you are born again you will never understand the Word of God." His words shocked me. I did not really know what he meant by being born again.

"I can read the Bible as well as you," I replied curtly.

However, I knew in my heart that I was not telling the truth, and this man's words stuck in my mind.

Billy Graham again visited our country a few years later. Again I went to hear him and listened to the same hymns and a similar message. I felt drawn to the front of the meeting, but again the same thoughts came to me — I was chairman of the stewardship council, a member of the vestry of the church, a secular adviser to the bishop. What would people think if I went to the front? Many of my friends went forward, but I refused to do so.

Again I went out of that meeting with a heavy heart.

The last thing I wanted was to have any real commitment towards God. I felt I was doing enough for Him. I thought of all the committees I was serving on to help God. It never occurred to me that I needed something more.

One day, as chairman of the Stewardship Council, I received a personal letter from one of the local parish committees. The substance of the letter was that the Stewardship Council was on the wrong track in its endeavours to raise money. The writer said that if people were committed to Jesus Christ they would give without being pressed to do so. He said we were driving people too hard.

These comments surprised me and I did not understand what he meant by saying that we should be committed to Jesus Christ.

I had barely put this matter out of my mind when a friend of mine, a chemist, told me that he and a group of friends were praying for me. This made me very uneasy. I could remember the days shortly after I commenced my law career, when a client, a Seventh-day Adventist, told me that both he and his church were praying for me. I didn't like this idea, as I felt that in some way they were trying to manipulate me.

Shortly afterwards my business partner, a member of the vestry of the local Anglican church, told me his vicar was encouraging children to speak in tongues. He asked me what I thought about it. I did not understand anything about the matter, but did recall that somewhere in the Bible it spoke about speaking in tongues on the Day of Pentecost. I was sure this phenomenon was not for today. As a lawyer I was very cautious so I told my friend I would report the matter to the bishop so he could discipline the vicar. I thought no more about the matter.

About that time, there were stirrings of charismatic renewal in the Anglican Church in New Zealand, though I personally had no knowledge of these matters.

But one person who was getting interested was my daughter, Maria, who was then 16. Maria and Pat went to a meeting in one of the local Anglican churches and when she arrived home her face was alight. I was reading a newspaper and she said to me, "Dad, you should have been there." I was not interested so continued reading my paper.

"Dad, you should have heard the man's testimony," she persisted. I knew what she meant by a testimony. People used to testify in the little church I had belonged to. I just grunted and made no further reply.

Then Maria said, "Dad, the man was a multi-millionaire." She had my immediate, absolute attention. I was always interested in people who had made money.

"Maria, how did he make his money?" I asked.

"By selling turkeys," she replied.

I thought that if everybody in New Zealand, which had a population of 3 million, ate turkeys every day, I could not make a million dollars out of that.

Then she told me that this man had talked in tongues. I was still unimpressed and said, "He must be a tongue talking turkey millionaire."

I had not realised that the man, Enoch Christoffersen, who was then in his late 60s, had come as part of an airlift to New Zealand with the Full Gospel Business Men's Fellowship.

He had given his testimony in that local Anglican church and Maria had been deeply impressed.

After the meeting she had bought a little booklet which she took home and read in her bedroom a few days later. She read that if she wanted to be born again of the Spirit of God, she needed to go on her knees, repent from her sins and ask Jesus Christ into her life. Maria was a sensitive child and did just that. As she did, the power of God filled the room.

She then turned to the next page of the booklet, which said if you wanted to be baptised in the Holy Spirit in the same way as the disciples were in the early church then simply ask Jesus Christ to do it.

Without any question in her mind Maria asked Jesus Christ to baptise her in the Holy Spirit and in the next few moments the power of God filled the room and she was speaking in tongues.

She left the room and told her mother of her experience and Pat immediately telephoned me in Dunedin, where I was sorting out some problems with Paul. She said something strange had happened to Maria and described the experience.

My first reaction was one of hurt pride. I had not yet got to the bishop to report the problem about the vicar getting the children to speak in tongues. Now my own daughter was doing so.

Then my reaction was parental concern. "If she continues to act strangely, call the doctor."

I arrived back in Auckland determined to sort out Maria, but found her a totally changed person. I decided to say nothing because her face was aglow and she seemed so responsive.

The next Sunday she wanted to go to church. This was a little unusual. From then on she went with us to church nearly every week.

I did not know that she had also begun to pray for her mother and father.

It is a dangerous thing when people begin to pray for others, and particularly for nominal Christians. Satan was perfectly happy with Bill Subritzky occupying all the offices he did in the church so long as his heart was not committed to God through Jesus Christ. So long as I was not born again, there was no problem.

However, with the possibility of this happening, Satan was obviously upset.

One way Satan operates is through miscommunication — and there were plenty of misunderstandings developing in our marriage. In the next nine months Pat and I grew colder towards one another to the point where separation was on its way.

At the end of nine months, another preacher, an Englishman, came to the same Anglican church. It was said that when he prayed for sick people they got healed. My family and some friends tried to encourage me to go but I was not interested.

"If he is all that good then take him down to the hospital. Let him pray for all the sick people and empty out the wards," I said.

However, I had some very persistent clients, some of whom were important people. One in particular kept ringing me and asking me to go.

Finally I could not avoid it, so one Saturday night Pat and I went to the meeting. We sat near the front.

Early in the meeting the preacher, Harry Greenwood, described an arthritic condition which he said was present in someone there. When he made that statement, one of my elderly clients walked out to the front. This dear old lady was full of arthritis and in extreme pain. I knew her well.

Harry Greenwood laid hands on her and said, "In the name of Jesus Christ I command you devil of sickness to leave this woman." As he did so, I thought he had hit her with an electric cattle prod. She jumped about half a metre in the air, shouted, her arms and legs straightened and she began to walk normally. All in the name of Jesus Christ. I could not believe my eyes or ears.

The preacher prayed for a number of other people and then preached an excellent sermon, and at the end made an appeal to those who wanted to give their lives to Jesus Christ.

Of course I knew this wasn't for me. I was chairman of the Stewardship Council, a secular adviser to the bishop, on the vestry and on many other committees. I dozed off and did not respond to any of the calls.

At the end of the meeting Pat said to me, "Bill, why don't we get our knees prayed for?" They had been damaged by skiing and it was apparent this man had some power, so I agreed to prayer so long as nobody saw us receiving it. We waited until 2am, when everybody had gone except the vicar, the preacher, Pat and myself.

Harry, a jovial man, stood in front of me and said, "Brother, what can I do for you?" I did not like that expression "brother". They did not use it in my church.

However, I described at length the problem we had in our knees. He listened very patiently.

When I had finished, he stood back, looked me up and down, and said, "Brother, if you spent more time on your knees you would have less problems." I could not believe my ears. I thought, "You cheeky Pom, are you telling me to pray?"

However, I let him pray for me and over the next two weeks the condition totally disappeared.

By now I was intrigued. I could see this man had a special power and he was a very likeable person. He had been a sailor, serving on the Ark Royal, and despite his riotous behaviour he had been gloriously saved. Thereafter, he studied as a preacher and evangelist and began to operate in the gifts of God.

I invited him to stay in my beach home at Stanmore Bay and he spent a couple of weeks there. When I visited him, he was not dressed like a preacher. He was in shorts and he invited me into the house and proceeded to tell me that he had borrowed my little yacht without my approval and broken its mast. I still liked him. We had a cup of tea together and I determined to go to one of his meetings in Hamilton, a city about 110 kilometres from Auckland.

However, I was not prepared to tell Pat I was going, so one night after dinner I walked out to my car without saying anything to her.

As I did so, Pat came out to her car as well. I asked where she was going and she said, "To Hamilton. Where are you going?"

Of course, I was going to Hamilton as well, so we went together.

The meeting was similar to the previous one. Harry had some excellent words of knowledge, calling people out of the audience with particular conditions and praying for them.

He again gave a message and at the end made a call for those who wanted to give their life to Jesus Christ.

I knew it was not for me. I was chairman of the Stewardship Council of the diocese, I was on the vestry of my church, I served on many other committees and I did not think it was necessary for me to go up and make a public demonstration of myself. So I ignored the call and waited impatiently for the end of the meeting.

On the way home I felt it would be good if we went to another meeting, even for the sake of our children. I tentatively asked Pat if she would be prepared to come the following night and she readily agreed.

All of our family were in Auckland, so the next night the six of us went.

We arrived early because I wanted to sit at the front to see exactly what Harry did as he prayed. He gave a good message and then came down the steps directly in front of me.

"The Lord has shown me that there is a young person in this meeting whose arm has been broken and it has been wrongly reset," he said.

There were about 1000 people in the hall. As soon as he had finished a young lad about 14 years of age ran from the back of the hall up to the front. The preacher laid hands on him and as he did so, his hands came down close to my face, touched the boy's arm and I heard the bones cracking as prayer for healing was given in the name of Jesus Christ. The arm was straightened and the boy ran back to his parents yelling, "I'm healed!"

Next the preacher called for a woman with a lump in the centre of her back. Before long a lady was standing directly in front of me, only about a metre away. As I watched, Harry placed his hand on the lump, then in the name of Jesus Christ said, "Go."

With that I watched the lump disappear in a flash.

I could not believe my eyes.

He went back on to the platform and began to preach again. Then he made a call to those who wanted to give their lives to Jesus Christ.

The same thoughts passed through my mind. I did not have to do such a thing because I already attended church, I was chairman of the Stewardship Council, I was a member of the vestry and all the other committees. So I did not move.

However, a new feeling was coming upon me, similar to the one I had felt in the Billy Graham meetings. I felt an urgent desire to respond to the call. Something in me was telling me to respond and something else was saying, "Don't be a fool." The battle grew stronger.

I felt like running but my children were beside me and if I got up and walked out it would seem I was a coward. I decided to stay there. The preacher carried on and he was very persistent. Fifteen minutes later he was still making his call for salvation.

Finally I felt I was going to explode if I did not do something. One part of me was saying to go forward and the other part was saying, "No."

When I could hold on no longer, I looked around and checked that every head was bowed and every eye closed. When I was sure this was so, I put my hand up and down in a flash. I don't think the preacher saw it, but God did.

Then I saw my family putting up their hands, and when Harry called for those who had done so to come forward we all did.

At the front of that meeting, in front of hundreds of people, our whole family prayed our way into the kingdom of God.

With that, the meeting concluded and I had almost reached the door when Maria stopped me, looked me in the eye and said, "Dad, why don't you come and get baptised in the Holy Spirit?"

"Not that tongues thing, Maria," I said lamely.

Pat then spoke, as though it was the last chance for our marriage, "Why don't we try it Bill?" I did not really want my marriage to fail and as Pat spoke these words she was expressing a hope with which I could identify.

Reluctantly I went to the back of the hall. There were tiered stairs and I sat in the third row up, surrounded by womenfolk and a few men. All our family were up there, except Maria, who was standing at the foot of the stairs, watching her father.

Harry Greenwood was praying for people. As he moved along and laid hands on them, some wept and others made strange sounds. I wanted to get out and run but Maria was looking at me. The preacher said, "Brother, in the name of Jesus Christ be baptised in the Holy Spirit. Open your mouth, brother, and speak out." Without thought, I did so and an unknown language poured out of me.

As this happened, Harry jumped in the air, his hands almost touching the ceiling, and shouted the loudest "hallelujah" I have ever heard. I am sure he thought God had cracked the toughest nut in New Zealand.

When it was time to go, I walked down the stairway and Maria approached me and said, "Dad you must feel different." I vaguely said, "Yes," but I was really quite bewildered.

The next morning I arose early and looked out of my bedroom window. I could not believe my eyes. I had never seen the grass so green, the trees so beautiful, nor heard the birds sing that way.

I ate breakfast, then drove to the office. As I looked at the sky, I realised I had never seen it so blue.

Then the words that my mother used to say to me came to my ears, "Except a man be born again he shall not enter the kingdom of God." I suddenly realised I was born again and was looking on the world as though I had entered it for the first time. My mother had died praying for me and now,

25 years later, her prayers were being answered.

My first thought was to tell somebody else about my experience. I parked my car and went to our office building. We were situated on the 11th floor, and on the way up I looked around the elevator to see who I could speak to about Jesus. A number of people were there and I waited until there was only one remaining as the others left the elevator at the various floors.

This person was another lawyer who was a close friend of mine and had served on many committees with me. He went on to become the Chief Justice of New Zealand.

I looked at him and said, "Ron, I want to tell you I've been born again and I speak in tongues." He looked completely startled and went out of the elevator with a strange look on his face.

When I reached my legal office, I called my two principal partners together and told them the wonderful news. They looked at each other, left the office and went down the corridor and had a conference.

Obviously I hadn't been very successful in sharing my faith, but I knew I could talk to Jesus. He was so real. I locked the office doors and went down on my knees and said, "Please, Jesus, do the same thing to my legal partners as You have done to me. And You had better start on that Catholic one. He will be the easiest!"

My Catholic partner, Terry Way, came to me about a week later and said he had been invited to a Catholic charismatic prayer meeting. I strongly recommended him to go. He attended the meeting for six weeks and at the end of that time rushed into the office shouting, "I've got it, I've got it." I knew he was born again of the Spirit of God and was baptised in the Holy Spirit.

Now there were two. We agreed to pray for our Anglican partner. He watched us for 18 months and at the end of that time came to a prayer meeting in my home. One night he went on his knees and received Jesus Christ as Lord and Saviour and was baptised in the Holy Spirit. Thereafter we had a Christian legal practice for 14 years.

I always said it was dangerous for people to come in for a divorce as they would be prayed right out of it. As a result of our testimonies, many people came to know the Lord during those years.

There were other dramatic results.

First of all, the peace of God came into our home. Our marriage was instantly healed. All darkness, distrust and failure went out of it, and from that moment on we have had an excellent marriage.

I found a wife I never knew existed. All the areas of reserve between us were broken and complete trust came into our relationship. I would never want to go back to the way we lived before.

Our children were also dramatically changed, especially Paul. The Paul we knew for the first eight years of his life returned. The rebellion, hate and anger disappeared as the soft, gentle person we knew as a child returned.

Subsequently I realised that what had happened in that bedroom in Stanmore Bay had been the result of a demonic entity living in that room. It had remained after sexual sin had been committed there. When Paul entered the room, it had attacked him and entered him because Pat and I were not fully committed as Christians and we did not know how to deal with the situation.

Over the years Paul had grown worse in his rebellion and attitude and this other entity had been working through him. In actual fact we had been dealing with a spiritual entity, not with our son.

Ephesians chapter 6 verse 12 says: "For we do not wrestle against flesh and blood, but against principalities, against powers, against the rulers of the darkness of this age, against spiritual hosts of wickedness in the heavenly places."

Now that Paul had been born again of the Spirit of God, the real Paul had returned. The false spirit which had entered him at the age of eight had disappeared. From thereon we have enjoyed a wonderful relationship with our son.

Janne and John were also born again of the Spirit of God and baptised in the Holy Spirit. Their lives were instantly changed for the better.

All our children have married Christians. Jesus Christ is the head of their homes. We also now have 11 grandchildren.

They all live in close proximity and each week we are home we have a family dinner, the whole 21 of us. The grandchildren love to come and many times will ring up to find out if it is family night.

Yes, one of the greatest blessings we can have is family life, and it has been a joy to watch our family grow and enjoy Christian marriages. Each of our children prayed for a Christian partner and God answered their prayers.

On March 10, 1971, Pat and I gave our lives to Jesus Christ and were born again of the Spirit of God and filled with the Holy Spirit. We did not realise just what a great adventure we had begun.

EIGHT

The Beginnings of Ministry

Barely three days after our born again experience, I had a strong impression that we should start a prayer meeting in our home. Interestingly enough, Pat had exactly the same impression, so we invited a few Christians to our home. About six gathered that first night. We did not really know what to do, but we prayed, sang a few hymns and somebody preached from the Bible.

From such a humble beginning, we decided to have a prayer meeting each Thursday night in our home. Soon a pianist offered her services and not long afterwards a friend, Doug Maskell, who attended a Baptist church and spoke in tongues, agreed to come and help us. Doug had considerable standing in the charismatic renewal, but he was not popular in his church because, at that time, Baptists were not responding to the baptism with the Holy Spirit and tongues.

The first night Doug attended our meeting he began to pray for individual people. I could not believe the insights he had concerning them. He gave them words of encouragement and told them how the Lord was dealing with their lives.

Because I had been born again under the ministry of a

preacher who moved in the gifts of the Holy Spirit, I was anxious to acquire these same gifts. I especially sought the word of knowledge, the word of wisdom, gifts of healing, the gift of faith and the gift of discerning of spirits.

I decided to stand alongside Doug at each meeting and see if I could catch some of his gift. Each night, before he prayed for a person, he asked what the Lord was saying to me about that person. My response was, “Nothing.” Then he would ask me if I felt the anointing of the Holy Spirit, and I would say, “No.”

Our meeting grew. Soon 50 people were attending, then 70, then 100 and more, with Doug still doing the same thing.

After nine months he had prayed for about 1500 people in this manner, and had asked me on each occasion whether the Lord was saying anything to me about the person concerned. The answer was always negative. Then he would ask me if I knew the anointing and I would say no again.

By now I was getting desperate. I seemed to be making no headway despite the fact that the prayer meetings were flourishing and prayers were being answered. Many people were coming back and testifying of the wonderful things God had been doing in their lives as a result of the meetings.

One night, in desperation, as Doug was asking me what the Lord was saying to me concerning a person, I began to speak out the impressions coming into my mind. He gave a great “hallelujah” and said, “I’ve got exactly the same thoughts.” Suddenly I felt a warm glow fall on me and knew it was the anointing of the Holy Spirit.

I was impatient to get to the next person, and again began to speak out the impressions I was receiving. Doug confirmed that he had the same impressions and we believed they were from the Lord. Again we knew this anointing.

That night I prayed for many people and the following Sunday went to my local Anglican church and asked the vicar to allow me to operate in the word of knowledge in the prayer meeting there. We had a sympathetic vicar who had also been attending the prayer meetings at our request.

That particular Sunday night I said I believed somebody in the group had a headache. Of course somebody did. Then I got the word "kidney" and asked whether anybody had a kidney problem. They all said no, but I persisted. After some time one of the people said, "I have just come from my sister's home and she is dying of a kidney disease." As I felt the anointing fall, I knew that God is not limited by time or space. That person had come to the prayer meeting with that concern. God was aware of it and wanted to demonstrate His knowledge.

From then on we began to move powerfully in the word of knowledge at the prayer meetings, while the Lord encouraged Pat into the gift of prophecy.

By now the meeting had grown very large, with several hundred attending. We used to clear out the various parts of our house and finally almost every room was filled with people. Even our basement was emptied and readied for the meeting.

Our gardeners took a full day to get the house ready and another day to take the chairs away and clean up afterwards.

One night the Holy Spirit seemed to say to me that there was a message in tongues which would come from the basement of our home. We had an intercommunication system throughout the house, together with closed-circuit television. I boldly stated that I believed somebody in the basement had a message in tongues. A few moments later a beautiful message flowed through the speaker system.

Then I said, "I believe the Holy Spirit has told me there is an interpretation of the message in the family room." Suddenly a beautiful interpretation flowed through the speaker system from that room.

The spirit of belief flooded the home and the anointing of God became very powerful.

Over the next eight years we held 48 meetings a year. Each year 7000 to 10,000 people attended, so over the eight years tens of thousands came. Thousands were born again of the Spirit of God and thousands were baptised in the Holy Spirit.

At the end of eight years, because of the large numbers attending, we moved to a public hall. A number of years later, we went to a larger hall. We are still holding these meetings in our home city.

Discovering the gifts of the Spirit in our home prayer meetings was a vital part of my early Christian growth.

Another important lesson I had to learn was the reality of demonic forces, and the Christian's authority over them through Jesus Christ.

Before being born again I had heard about superstitious tribes in Africa and Papua New Guinea which were involved with demons but I didn't believe they existed in modern Western cultures.

We had been conducting our home meetings only a short time when our vicar brought along a man who had a problem. He was about 40 and when he began to sing in tongues a voice seemed to take over and he could not stop. We did not know what to do about it.

At the conclusion of the meeting we went to my study and began to pray for the man. Nothing in particular was happening, but suddenly the word "abortion" came into my mind. I spoke that word out and as soon as I did so the man fell on the floor, curled up like a foetus and began to scream. I had met my first demon.

We prayed for this man for several hours until early in the morning. Suddenly he looked out of the window and, with his eyes bulging, a voice said, "They're everywhere, they're everywhere." I thought it was referring to other demons.

As he was still not set free, we decided to take him to the church for a communion service, even though it was 3am. As we went out to the car, the same voice was shouting, "They're everywhere, they're everywhere."

We went to the church and prayed for him and then had communion. He was still not delivered.

The following week he came again and we went through much the same procedure. This happened for a number of weeks until finally, with a great rush and scream, the demon left him.

I thought no more of the matter until a few weeks later when I was driving along the motorway and the Lord reminded me of the incident.

"I want you to know that when he said, 'They're everywhere,' it was not demons he was speaking about, but angels surrounding your house. This is what the demon in the man was looking at."

I rejoiced greatly when the Lord told me this.

A few weeks later a reporter from the New Zealand

Broadcasting Corporation came to one of the prayer meetings. He sat through the meeting and afterwards asked me some questions. He came back the next morning, and while he was speaking with me, the Holy Spirit said to me, "This man wants to know Me." I asked the young man if this was so and he said, "Yes, I do want to know Jesus." He went on his knees repented and I led him to the Lord.

After he made his commitment demonic powers began to manifest out of him. I prayed for him for some time and suddenly a similar voice to that which had spoken out of the first man spoke out of him. The man was looking out the window and the voice was saying, "They're everywhere, they're everywhere."

This time I knew what the demon was looking at. I said, "Yes, demon, they are angels aren't they?"

The demon voice responded, trembling through the man, "Yes, yes, yes, they are angels." Then the demons fled and the man was completely free.

I believe that as we minister, with full belief in Jesus Christ, in the deliverance ministry, that ministering angels surround and protect us, our home and family.

As the years went by we came across many cases requiring deliverance. We often prayed for these people after the meetings and sometimes it took several hours for them to be delivered. The family began to call my study the zoo because of the strange noises that came from it. People barked, roared like lions, screamed, shouted and made all sorts of weird sounds.

One day I was praying in the study with a man and he began to bark like a dog. The housekeeper could hear the dog barking, so she rushed through the house with a broom trying to find it. Needless to say, she never did.

We also found that strange things would happen to our cat. She was a very peaceful animal and would sleep quietly during the prayer meetings. However, when demons began to manifest and we were casting them out, she would spin like a top. We realised the demons were leaving the people and going into the cat. So we cast the demons out of the cat and she would return to her peaceful state.

As we began to learn more, we found great miracles were happening.

One night a lady who was riddled with cancer and had 14 other complaints came to the meeting. The Lord gave me a word of knowledge for her during the meeting, but she failed to respond because she was too embarrassed.

Afterwards she came to me for prayer. I told her that the Holy Spirit showed me that her heart was full of unforgiveness and that she should go home and for the next week forgive every person who had ever hurt her. She was somewhat mystified by this response, but during the next week she forgave many people.

She came to the next meeting and we prayed for her. Nothing happened immediately, but she continued to come each week for the next year.

During that year every one of the 14 complaints disappeared from her body and her cancer was totally healed. Nineteen years later that lady still testifies of the miraculous healing that took place in her life. She runs a business, works 80 hours a week and has the energy of a person 20 years younger than herself.

Hundreds of such testimonies came out of the meetings. Many people said that when they walked through the front door of our home, they felt the tremendous peace and love of God. As that peace came on them, they came into a knowledge of Jesus Christ and, later in the meeting, they would give their lives to Him.

NINE

The Best Bible College

I had been born again under the ministry of a man with a real gift of evangelism, Harry Greenwood. I soon realised that I had an abysmal knowledge of the Bible. God immediately gave me a hunger for His Word and I began to read it almost ravenously.

I had recalled that when I studied law, I had to learn nearly a thousand cases for each of the 18 subjects for which I had to pass examinations. I had to learn the names of the parties, the facts of the case and the decision in each case. I felt that if I had to give that amount of study to learn how to become a lawyer, I certainly should be prepared to give an equivalent effort in my study of the Word of God.

Ever since I have been born again I have read the Bible each morning by a method that takes me through the Old Testament about six times a year and the New Testament about 30 times a year. I found that by reading it in this manner, God has blessed me greatly with an understanding of His Word. Whatever I did not understand I simply believed. Over a period of time the Holy Spirit has given me an understanding of many passages which I found difficult in my early days as a Christian.

Shortly after I was born again, I was fortunate to sit under the ministry of a world-famous Bible teacher, Dr Derek Prince. Dr Prince had been a King's Scholar at Eton College, Cambridge, and was also a fellow of King's College, Cambridge. He has an extraordinary testimony of how, as a philosopher, God met him mightily during the desert war in North Africa and transformed his life. He met his first wife, Lydia, at that time.

I was immediately attracted to Derek's incisive mind and clear manner of teaching. It appealed to me very greatly because of my own legal training. I could see that his messages were orderly, well-researched and thoroughly Biblical.

I began listening to his teaching tapes and for the first five years of my Christian walk I spent innumerable hours listening to his teaching. I learnt many of his tapes by heart. I had them transcribed so that I could better understand them and absorb them thoroughly into my spirit.

Since I have been a Christian, I have listened to hundreds of Bible teachers, but I have never found a teacher with such a clear, yet simple, understanding of the Word of God. Nor have I heard the word expounded in such a scholarly way, nor have I found a teacher of greater integrity. Dr Prince has been a gift from God to tens of millions throughout the world as his radio broadcasts have been expanded.

Dr Prince opened the Bible to me as no other man could. I will be forever indebted to him.

I thank God daily that He raised such a man up. I have been able to preach in hundreds of crusade meetings with a knowledge that my message has been solidly founded on the Word of God and with a confidence that has been born out of years of listening to Bible exposition from Dr Prince.

I have mentioned his first wife, Lydia. She also was a remarkable woman who called a spade a spade. She never wasted words and stood by her Christian principles through thick and thin despite much persecution.

Lydia Prince passed to be with the Lord in 1975. She was speaking in tongues as she left this world!

Some years later, Derek Prince married his second wife, Ruth. She is a delightful person with a deep sense of the knowledge and presence of God.

It has indeed been an honour and privilege to have known Derek Prince over these years. He is truly one of God's generals who has influenced millions of lives worldwide as he has fearlessly proclaimed the good news of Jesus Christ and at the same time equipped the saints for the work of the ministry.

TEN

God in the Workplace

My relationship with God also brought me into a completely different sphere as far as my businesses were concerned.

Whereas previously my companies had been built up by my own efforts, I could now ask God how I should act, what I should do and where I should turn. I often shut my office door to pray for guidance, and would always receive it.

During the 1970s, there was a burst of immigration into the country and our house building business expanded as never before. As we depended on land supply for home building, I bought more and more property around Auckland city and we were able to build thousands of homes. It seemed the good times would never end, but I was due for a shock.

By 1975 the oil shock had affected Western countries and our Government was beginning to borrow money from overseas to maintain employment. But at the end of the year there was a change back to a conservative government.

In those days 90 per cent of finance for housing came from the Government, which controlled the money supply.

If it wanted to have a boom it let the money supply go and if it wanted to restrict things it reined in that supply. Before each election, the money supply would expand and building would boom, but afterwards it would be restricted for the next year or so.

However, after this particular change of government, rather than a restriction of money, there was a total cut-off. Suddenly there was no loan money available for three months. Our business was brought to a standstill and we had to wait until the new budget was issued by the Minister of Finance.

I was overseas when I telephoned New Zealand to learn its contents and was shocked to hear that loans had been reduced by $5000 each. As we dealt with people who had very little deposit for their home, this meant there would be a much greater loan gap to be bridged. I had a very restless night, not knowing what the future would hold. I was facing many problems because of my heavy land commitments and mortgage obligations.

As I prayed about it, however, I seemed to get a clear understanding that I should approach a major finance institution and persuade it to issue second mortgages to bridge the gap. For a number of years we had been dealing with a major finance house which had given small second mortgages for our clients, but now it was obvious that I had to ask it for large mortgages.

When I returned to New Zealand, I approached the directors of that institution and, after proper consideration, they agreed to grant the second mortgages. No other company had access to such finance and the Lord blessed me and enabled me to maintain the company. Later, as we approached another election, the circumstances changed again and the Government freed up the financial restraints.

However, I had clearly seen the hand of the Lord in all of this. As a precaution against further loan cutting by the Government, I approached an Australian finance institution which agreed to advance $2 million to our company. We did not need the money immediately, but I wanted it available in case things became difficult. Sure enough, about a year later, the money supply was extremely tight. No finance could be raised and I was grateful that I had this $2 million in the bank. It was a useful insurance during this very difficult period.

Again the Lord was blessing me.

Part of my business philosophy has always been to keep abreast of technological advancements.

When dictaphones were invented, they completely revolutionised my work style as they meant I could work at night, dictating many letters which could be typed the next day.

Another major advancement was the advent of the computer, and when I became convinced of the value of computerisation I got into it boots and all.

Initially, when a major computer distributor approached our legal office and suggested that we turn over our accounting system to computers, I rejected the idea because we had a very efficient bookkeeping system.

Shortly afterwards, however, the lady in charge of the system resigned and our bookkeeping fell into chaos. I therefore called my partners together and suggested that we took a further look at the computer system.

The computer specialists told us only one other legal office had computerised its accounts, and that it had maintained its old accounting system alongside the computer system for a year in case the computer system broke down.

They estimated it would take nine months to set up our system, and if it was going to be done more quickly, it would need a person to act like a dictator in the office to ensure all the systems were properly controlled.

Such a delay was clearly unsatisfactory given the fact that our existing system was falling apart.

While the specialists were present, I called a printer and asked how long it would take to print our stationery. He said he could have it by the following week.

I then asked the specialists how long it would take them to have their program ready. They said it could be available very quickly, but were astonished at the speed with which I wanted the system installed. It was less than three weeks before Christmas and I wanted the system fully operational by February 1, even though the legal office would be closed during January.

They did not think it was possible, but towards the end of January they moved in with their equipment. By then all the stationery had been printed and the systems were ready.

My partners agreed I should be the dictator.

On January 31, every file was taken out and given a number. We worked throughout the weekend, changing over thousands of files into the system, and on February 1 we started with the computers. I sat in the office and controlled the system each day. Everybody had to fill in the correct forms daily so they were ready for the computer program. Because of the conservative attitudes of legal firms, this proved difficult. In order to encourage accuracy, I presented a lemon each day to the person who made the most mistakes in filling in their forms.

After a few days, I abandoned the old bookkeeping system and relied on computers. The system never failed and we became the first legal firm in New Zealand to be totally computerised.

By now some of my staff in the housing company were pressing me to install a computer there. I did not immediately see the advantage of doing so, but agreed that we should go ahead. We employed three programmers and began to program our systems.

Once I saw the benefits of the computer I was constantly suggesting new programs. It was not long before our total accounting system was on computer.

Then we looked at our costing system, which we had worked on over a number of years. It is vital to have a top-class costing system in a building company where even the smallest error on each unit can make the difference between profit and loss on a house.

We had a reasonably efficient system, but when we placed it on computer it rapidly became more sophisticated.

Each day I was given the costing of every house and a print-out showing the errors on each component. It meant that at a glance I could see the profit and loss on each house. If our costing staff had underestimated any item, it clearly showed up. The same occurred if they had overestimated.

Soon we perfected the system so we could build a house within one half of one per cent of estimate. We allowed this amount of tolerance in the costing system. If the invoice for an item exceeded the estimate by half a per cent, the computer rejected the invoice.

We were also able to control thefts from the jobs. Each carpentry gang was assigned to a particular house and we soon found out whether there was a pattern of thefts occurring with the same gang.

Our telephone calls were also monitored by computer. Every enquiry from a possible purchaser came through our 14-line phone system. Previously our salespeople had been allowed to receive sales enquiries in their homes, but now I forbade this. Instead I set up a system whereby our telephones were manned from 7am until 11pm each day. In this way, instead of an enquiry being answered by a salesman's wife or child, it was answered by a skilled operator at our office.

To advertise our houses, we filled the newspaper with small "scatter" advertisements. We found that people buying homes looked at small advertisements rather than large ones. Sometimes one person would ring four or five of our numbers not realising they were speaking to the same company.

Every telephone call was logged and we could immediately tell the effectiveness of each advertisement. We could then become cost-efficient in our advertising. If an advertisement was not bringing results, it was promptly changed.

Each salesman had to produce his own advertisements each week, so we could soon tell whether or not they were effective.

We soon discovered that television and radio advertising were ineffective, and ultimately 90 per cent of our enquiries came from scatter advertisements.

The system became so efficient that if a salesman's girlfriend called in, her name and address were logged. Each day we knew exactly the number of enquiries we had received and could relate these enquiries back to the salesman. We knew that it took a certain number of enquiries for the average salesman to effect a sale. If he did not do so then we knew there was something wrong with his selling methods.

Similarly, we began to design our houses on computer.

Over a four-year period, our total operations were thoroughly computerised. Soon we had in excess of 600 programs. The IBM representative told me he had never seen a computer used for so many programs.

The computer became the key to our success and expansion.

On occasions the Minister of Housing visited our premises and I was able to show him the number of enquiries we were receiving and the large number we could not satisfy because of lack of finance. On one occasion he quoted in Parliament all the statistics we had given him.

The computer also proved crucial to our expansion programme into branches. Previously it had been impossible to cost accurately in areas outside Auckland, but now we were able to call for quotes for each component from many suppliers. These were fed into the computer and it would select the cheapest supplier for each component and place the orders.

We began to build homes in the most difficult localities, establishing 14 branches in all in response to a word from the Lord.

One reason for establishing the branches was that the price of the sections on which we built our homes had fallen considerably.

The industry was again going through a recession and it was pointless to develop our own land in Auckland because the cost of development exceeded the sale price of the sections.

We then thought of listing every available section in the

Auckland area. We went to all the land agents and promised they could keep their commission if they gave us the listing of the sections. We soon had 8000 sections listed throughout metropolitan Auckland, grouping them in price ranges. We were thus able to instantly direct a prospective purchaser to one of these sections. Our salesmen were also supplied with plans of these sections and any details concerning difficulties in building on them.

At this time our land bank was little use because we could not develop the sections as cheaply as those that were available on the market. Thus we were able to draw on the supply of sections belonging to other people.

When we had a suitable purchaser for a section, we entered into a contract to buy it on the condition that the purchasers would get a loan on their house. When the loan was granted, we completed the purchase of the section on behalf of our buyer and sold it on at the same price.

In this way we were able to overcome the problem of supply of sections. We had the best listings in Auckland.

We extended the same principle to each town where we had branches. These branches carried on over the next six years until the supply of sections in their area was exhausted. By then land values had increased and our land bank was again valuable. Now it became profitable for us to develop sections on our own land and sell these.

One day, while I was preparing to go to Sydney on ministry, one of my staff reported that our computer had broken down.

For two days the staff had been trying to get it to function and IBM had sent messages world-wide to ascertain the cause of the problem. So far there had been no success.

Because we totally relied on this computer, the position was desperate. Later we installed a new system which obviated this, but at that stage we had no back-up.

I knew I could not go to Sydney and leave this problem. During the lunch hour I went down to the computer room and when nobody was present, laid hands on the computer and prayed over it. I said nothing.

After lunch the staff went to get the computer fixed. When they started using it, it worked perfectly. They rushed up to tell me what had happened. I then told them I had prayed for it.

I was able to take my trip to Sydney with complete peace of mind.

On another occasion, I was in the United States when I received an urgent call from my general manager.

The housing industry had expected some relief in the budget but that had not been forthcoming.

Although we had access to second mortgage funds, these were not enough to ward off a recession. My general manager told me I should return immediately because the company was facing a crisis.

I had been aware for some time that our sales had been declining, but was confident the Government would do something to help the building industry. That help did not, in fact, come until early the following year, which was an election year. In the meantime many of our competitors were collapsing and our sales were very poor.

I resolved to move my office from my legal company into the housing company and to stay there until the crisis was resolved. Little did I realise that I would be there for the next seven years.

My first move was to expand our advertising. I called in

the best advertising agents and at the same time decided on a large-scale programme of display homes. These were very bold moves and cost a lot of money, but there was no alternative.

We rapidly built several display home villages around Auckland.

In addition, I met with our 14 salespeople each day and spent a lot of time encouraging them. Each month I promulgated a number of new sales incentives which were offered to all our clients.

We allied ourselves with major furniture companies, who agreed to supply carpeting, curtains, blinds and articles of furniture at reduced rates. They were also suffering a recession and were only too glad to join forces with us.

We were able to offer a complete programme of furnishing homes on a minimum deposit and with repayments spread over a long term.

In addition, we offered fences, paths and lawns at a very low deposit and low repayments.

As soon as the sales force realised that I had taken the initiative and was putting my whole effort into the organisation, our sales improved markedly.

In that first year we spent over $1 million in advertising.

Then a major newspaper approached us saying it would give us a large amount of advertising space if we would donate a house to a competition. We agreed and for six months the paper ran stories on our operations and gave us considerable publicity.

All these measures increased our sales substantially and the morale of our sales force improved 100 per cent.

The next hurdle to overcome came when the Government changed its policies so that low-interest loans could be given for the purchase of older houses as well as new ones. This meant that for the first time in 25 years, we had to compete with the used house market.

We developed a programme whereby we could prove to home buyers that it was better for them to buy a new home than a used one. We produced a five-year guarantee, and we continued to outsell the opposition.

Although used homes were up to $25,000 cheaper, I knew they would rise in price as finance was made available for them. Once we had weathered the initial opposition, we were all right.

Throughout the next seven years, I was at the office every day and was not involved in ministry outside of Auckland. I spent most of my time walking around the office checking our systems on a daily or even hourly basis. In this way our company forged ahead during some of the most difficult times ever faced by the building industry in New Zealand.

For example, one year when all the other companies suffered a decline in sales, ours increased by 50 per cent.

By encouraging our staff and taking a personal interest in each of them we found that many remained with the company for up to 25 years. From the managing director downwards, they were extremely loyal.

Although we had extended credit arrangements with some suppliers, we always endeavoured to keep our financial payments on time. In this way we maintained the confidence of our suppliers and were able to get the keenest deals. If we realised we would be late with a payment, we rang the supplier and explained why.

Many Christian organisations held meetings in our board room during this period and this resulted in much prayer for our company, staff members and clients. I always found it a blessing to open the premises for uses other than business and over the years many decisions important to the Christian community were made in our offices.

A major reason our business was so successful was that we always paid attention to the customer.

I learned early in my legal career that people want service and I built my legal practice by providing service to my clients even though, at times, this was at considerable personal cost.

We applied the same principle, namely that the customer is always right, in building houses. No matter what complaints people made about their home we would fix them. It took months to satisfy some people, but we ensured all their complaints were attended to.

Sometimes our building supervisors would become extremely frustrated dealing with the most difficult people, but we would tell them to keep going back until they were satisfied.

One woman claimed her house was about a metre out of position. She wanted substantial compensation. We knew she really wanted the money because the siting of the house did not inconvenience her at all.

We would not pay her, so we decided to move the house. It had to be completely repainted and wallpapered and a great deal of structural work was required.

Despite such unreasonable people we persisted in our approach. For many years I employed a person to go round and see the homes we had built. Some months after the owners had taken residence, we asked them to give a quality report on their home. This proved very enlightening and we were able to eliminate a lot of problems and build better houses.

In dealing with bank managers, I maintained a policy of total integrity.

On occasions, when our annual accounts were reviewed, corporate officers from the head office of the bank would be concerned about the amount of finance we required. However, I would carefully detail our plans and, so far as possible, ensure these were accomplished. In this way we established confidence with our bank.

This approach paid off handsomely as we often obtained finance from our bank when our competitors could not.

As a Christian I naturally was favourably disposed towards employing other Christians. However, I found that this did not always work out.

Sometimes I found Christians would forget the master-servant relationship and treat me as a brother in the Lord rather than as their master during working hours. Of course they were Christian brothers, but there was also a master-servant relationship involved and this had to take priority during working hours.

Some Christians would bypass all the officers of the company and come direct to me with their problems or ideas. This caused great resentment among the staff.

I told one of our Christian salesmen that I felt he was not conducting himself properly as a Christian. He disagreed with me, so I suggested that we went together and saw his pastor. He refused to do this, but instead went to eight other pastors and gave them his version of the story. He then came back and told me I was the one who needed to be disciplined.

Subsequently this man commenced his own company, which he publicly proclaimed as a Christian building company. About two years later it collapsed in financial ruin.

I became very wary about employing people who called themselves Christians. I found that many come to the Lord, but are not obedient to His Word. No one is perfect in this regard, but it becomes very difficult when people say they are Christians and yet are totally disobedient to the Word of God.

On the other hand, I employed some wonderful Christians over the years and was always grateful for their integrity, honesty and support.

During the last 10 years that I owned the company, a Bible was given to every home purchaser as they took possession. This meant we had to maintain the highest standard of integrity with our clients.

We had a number of testimonies from people who gave their lives to the Lord as a result of reading their Bible.

I am sure that over the years our stand on some of these issues contributed greatly to our success. Certainly the 14,000 families who purchased our homes over the years must have agreed.

ELEVEN

Miracles In Ministry

Over the years, I managed to somehow balance business commitments with increasing opportunities to minister both overseas and in New Zealand.

Strangely enough, one of my earliest overseas ministry opportunities came through my political contacts, not my business or church associations.

It came after my friend, Warren Freer, with whom I had shared a platform many years before during his first election campaign, introduced me to the Leader of the Opposition, Norman Kirk.

I found him a very sincere person and quite frequently when he was in Auckland he visited me at my office. I was able to testify to him about my walk with Jesus Christ and one day, in the presence of others, he knelt down and gave his life to the Lord. A few months later he became Prime Minister of New Zealand.

About this time I learned that the Anglican Church in Fiji was beginning to undergo renewal. I was told the church would like to receive literature, so I arranged for two cartons of Christian books to be sent to Suva and I thought no more about the matter.

Pat and I took a holiday in Fiji each year, but we never went to Suva because that part of the country was always very wet. We preferred the western end of the island because it is much drier.

On this particular occasion, while we were preparing to go to Fiji, somebody suggested that I go to Suva and pray for people there. By now our prayer meeting had been going nearly a year and we were becoming quite well known.

I rejected this suggestion because I did not want to go to wet Suva, and thought no more about the matter. However, a few days before we were due to leave, Norman Kirk rang me and said, "Bill, I hear you are going to Fiji. As you know, there was a cyclone there a few months ago and I want our Government to help out in the best way possible. I will give you diplomatic authority to meet the Prime Minister of Fiji and discuss the problem with him. I will also tell the armed forces to be available to take you to the various parts of Fiji and check out the damage."

Who was I to refuse such a request from our Prime Minister?

This, of course, meant I had to go to Suva after all. The Lord has wonderful ways of arranging things.

While there I enquired about the local Anglican church and contacted Father Edward Subramani, who came to our hotel to meet Pat and me. There we prayed for him to receive the baptism of the Holy Spirit and I gave him a book by the Rev Dennis Bennett called "Nine O'clock in the Morning".

About two months later, Father Subramani attended a meeting of the World Council of Churches in Bangkok. While there, he went for a bus trip during which he sat alongside the Bishop of Singapore, Bishop Chiu.

The bishop indicated that he felt quite dry spiritually and Father Subramani gave him the book by Dennis Bennett to read.

Bishop Chiu went to his hotel and lay down for an afternoon nap. First of all, however, he read the book and prayed, "Lord if you can baptise Dennis Bennett with the Holy Spirit and give him the gift of tongues, you can do that also to me." Then he fell asleep.

When he awoke, he was speaking in tongues.

Some years later, as part of an increasing involvement in overseas ministry, I was invited by Bishop Chiu to conduct crusades in the Singapore Cathedral.

During these crusades, he asked me to teach on demonology and when I was in the cathedral I realised there were demonic powers within it.

However, I did not feel it was proper for me to say anything to the bishop, but left it to the Lord to reveal it to him.

As I was conducting the class on demonology with the clergy, the bishop interrupted me and said, "Bill, I believe we have demons in our cathedral." I agreed with him.

At that moment the Lord gave me a vision of a dark angel about two metres high, situated on the spire of the cathedral. I shared this with the bishop, who had no difficulty believing it because during the war the Japanese brought many Australian nurses into the grounds of the cathedral and massacred them and buried them there.

We decided to form a procession and march around the cathedral in a similar way as the Bible describes the march around the city of Jericho. All the clergy participated in the procession and the bishop and I led it.

As we walked past the area where the nurses had been buried, there was a sound like a rushing wind from the spire of the cathedral as God drove off the demonic powers.

We prayed and marched. The wind of the Spirit came down and took Bishop Chiu to the ground. He had not previously fallen under the power of the Spirit and did not understand what was happening to him.

Afterwards we went into the cathedral and, in the name of Jesus Christ, cleansed it.

Since then the Singapore diocese has experienced tremendous spiritual growth. There could be other reasons for this, but I believe the cleansing of the cathedral and the removal of that angel played a significant part in this development.

This was the first of a number of times I have been asked to pray for the cleansing of churches from demonic power.

Usually I go to the four corners of the building and lay hands on them, commanding any demonic powers to flee. On one occasion, as I did so, I walked past a window on the outside of the church and the Holy Spirit said to me, "Spirit of larceny." I commanded that spirit to depart.

The vicar then told me that the church treasurer had been indicted for stealing the church funds! His office had been in the room where that window was.

I then went into the centre of the church and the Holy Spirit showed me an unseen well in the ground. The church had been built over an old Maori burial ground and I saw clearly how demon powers were rising up out of that well and into the church. We closed off that entry point and cleansed the building.

Subsequently the vicar reported a great increase in membership of the church.

On another occasion, as a vicar and I walked past the front of the altar, the Holy Spirit said, "Command the spirit of murder to leave."

I did so, and the vicar told me that one of the members

of the vestry had been charged with murder. While he was on bail awaiting trial, he rebuilt the floor in front of the altar. Obviously he had left the spirit of murder behind him.

We must always be aware of the tremendous power in the name and blood of Jesus Christ. We must also be aware of the way in which the enemy seeks to attack and invade. As we follow the Holy Spirit, we can be assured of God's protection and love, as well as His cleansing power in every circumstance.

In cleansing the Singapore Cathedral we helped free the Anglican churches there to grow significantly.

Singapore was the first Anglican diocese in the world in which every European church experienced renewal. Fourteen such churches have been renewed in the Spirit. The last time I was in Singapore, all these churches were crowded with converts and the Spirit of God was moving mightily.

It is amazing how God uses people and events for His purposes.

Norman Kirk's invitation to go to Suva resulted in me meeting Edward Subramani which resulted in Bishop Chiu's renewal and the renewal of the Anglican Church in Singapore.

On another occasion, while I was teaching at a charismatic conference in Suva, I noticed an older European man, sitting in the front row. He was dressed in jeans, wearing jandals and had an open-necked shirt.

Somebody whispered to me, "That is Derek Rawcliffe, the Bishop of the New Hebrides (now called Vanuatu)."

It was the first time I had seen a bishop so casually dressed.

During the conference, Bishop Rawcliffe asked me to go

to the New Hebrides and conduct a seminar for his clergy. Six months later, Pat and I flew to Port Vila, the first time we had returned there since my involvement in the shipping line many years earlier.

I found the place had been completely changed into a modern, bustling seaport.

The Christians who met us said they had been praying and fasting for their nation, which had been the subject of British and French joint rule for 50 years, but was about to celebrate independence.

When I arrived, the Lord gave me a vision of a great creature over the nation facing towards the south. It had hair like a goat, a nose like a horse, ears like a giraffe and a head like a bear. Under it was written the word "division".

It did not take me long to realise that this was one of the spiritual strongmen placed over that nation by Satan, and that the country was facing division and bloodshed.

As soon as we arrived, we were taken to meet the Prime Minister. He was very gracious and after a few minutes began to tell us about a dream he had had three years earlier.

He took about 20 minutes to explain this dream, and then he looked at me expectantly as though I could interpret it for him. I said to the Lord, "I am not a Daniel or a Joseph." However, He began to give me the interpretation and for the next 15 minutes I spoke it out.

This event was significant in relation to other things that happened during our stay.

Bishop Rawcliffe contacted me shortly after my arrival and said he now doubted whether it was wise for me to speak to the synod, as he did not think it was quite ready for me.

However, the following Monday morning, as the Prime Minister opened the synod, he said something like this:

"Members of the synod will know that three years ago I had a dream and I have visited every pastor, priest or minister in this country whom I can possibly find in order to give me an interpretation of that dream. So far I have never had that interpretation. Now a man called Mr Subritzky has visited this country and, last Saturday, gave me the interpretation of that dream."

This statement by the Prime Minister meant the synod was prepared to listen to me.

The following Saturday, I taught the 90 members of the synod on demonology and then, on the Sunday, spoke on baptism with the Holy Spirit and salvation generally.

One of those attending was Father Walter Lini, the head of the People's Revolutionary Movement, which had been elected to run the government, but which the British and French would not allow to take office.

This movement had control of the countryside, while the government controlled the towns. During the synod, Father Lini went out from time to time to contact his forces and give them directions.

On the Sunday afternoon, when the time came for us to minister the baptism of the Holy Spirit, the bishop, together with Pat and myself, laid hands on all the members of the synod. All of them came into the gift of tongues.

Then we prayed for each one to receive gifts of the Holy Spirit and the first man to speak out a message in a public tongue was Father Lini.

Subsequently he became Prime Minister of that nation without any bloodshed. I am sure that the prayers of the churches, plus the fact that the Christians had stood against the demonic power that was over the nation, allowed God to move in a mighty way. Through prayer and fasting, the Christians had brought down that strongman.

One result of that synod was that the clergy became renewed in the Spirit. Many went back to their churches and, instead of their normal Sunday night evensong, preached the Gospel with renewed fire and vigour. Many of their people were baptised with the Spirit. They began to pray for the sick and cast out demons. Some of the services went until 1 o'clock the next morning.

This renewal then spread up into the Solomon Islands, north of Vanuatu.

During our visit, Bishop Rawcliffe took me to the local hospital, where we met the superintendent.

He had seen me operate in the word of knowledge and took me around the wards and asked me to comment on the condition of the various patients. As the Lord gave me words of knowledge concerning their condition, he would remove the chart on the wall above each patient and compare them. He was amazed at the accuracy of the word of knowledge.

By the time we reached the seventh patient, I said to him, "Those are the things that you already have on your chart, but I will show you additional things that I believe the Lord is telling me."

We went around the entire ward and the man was clearly impressed by the power of the Holy Spirit.

That night he came to the meeting. He was a very large man and when he fell under the power of the Spirit, he was wedged in the doorway for a considerable time. God has a wonderful way of moving upon people.

I also preached at a Presbyterian church, and as I stood up to speak the Holy Spirit told me that 13 people in that church were committing adultery. I spoke this out and asked for these people to come forward. Immediately 13 did and I led them into repentance.

During another very large meeting, the Holy Spirit gave me a specific word that there was a person sitting near the back of the meeting who had a bowel condition.

I spoke out this word of knowledge but nobody responded. I persisted, but still nobody responded. Four times I walked down the aisle to the back of the meeting, and each time pointed to the person to whom I believed the Lord was directing me. The man did not move.

On the fifth occasion, as I pointed to him and began to walk back up the hallway, he followed me. As he came to the front, the power of God fell on him and he spent the next hour on the floor.

At the end of the meeting he stood up, tears streaming from his eyes. He said he had been about to go to New Zealand for an operation on a bowel condition which he had had for over 13 years. He now knew he was healed.

Interestingly, he was the Session Clerk of the Presbyterian Church. He told me he had been actively opposed to charismatic renewal, but now he had seen the power of God his viewpoint had changed. He promised that on the next Sunday morning, he would stand up in his church and proclaim that God was really involved in the charismatic renewal and that he was repenting from his previous stand on this matter.

I subsequently learned that real renewal took place in that Presbyterian church.

Shortly afterwards, I was invited back to Fiji, where I conducted a crusade in the Suva Cathedral. Among the crowds were Fijians and Indians, many of whom were Hindus and Muslims.

A large number come to such meetings because they want to be healed. Jesus Christ used healing and deliverance in His own ministry and encouraged His disciples to do likewise. When people see signs and wonders, they crowd into the meetings.

One afternoon, as I was preparing for the meeting, I read a magazine which featured the Hindu goddess Dirga. I thought nothing more of the matter, but that evening when I was preaching, the Holy Spirit interrupted me and said, "Command the goddess Dirga to loosen her grip over these people."

I stopped preaching and said, "In the name of Jesus Christ, I command you goddess Dirga to release your grip over these people." I kept repeating it. Within a few moments, many of the Hindus had fallen to the ground and were writhing like snakes. Most were moving over the pews and wriggling under them at an incredible speed. The noise was unbelievable. I kept speaking for five minutes and by then about a hundred people were manifesting demonic power.

When the Holy Spirit said, "Stop," I asked the eight Anglican clergy who had been taught how to minister in deliverance to step forward and pray for these people. Gradually the noise subsided and the manifestations ceased.

I then resumed my message. When I made an appeal for salvation at the end of the message, about 150 people came forward, most of them Hindus and Muslims. They had seen a power manifest which was much greater than any of their gods. In fact, they had seen their own gods submit to the power of the name of Jesus Christ.

Over the years I have had the opportunity to minister in many parts of the world, but perhaps my various visits to

Papua New Guinea stand out as the most outstanding examples of God moving in sovereign power.

On one visit, we opened with meetings in Port Moresby and Lae, and were set to finish off in Rabaul.

In Port Moresby, after the call for salvation, I prayed for the Holy Spirit to fall on the thousand people gathered before the platform. He fell in a mighty way and all began to talk in tongues. They raised their hands to God and stood transfixed under the power of the Holy Spirit for 45 minutes.

In Lae, there had been rains for some weeks before our arrival. The rains stopped on the nights of our crusades, then started again when we left.

In Rabaul, as the opening choruses finished, I stepped down as usual to pray for the sick by the word of knowledge.

I walked towards those seated on the ground and felt the Holy Spirit direct me to a man to pray for his eyesight. The man stood and as I prayed, he immediately fell under the power of the Spirit. A few minutes later he stood up and began to look around.

I said to the person beside him, "What is going on?"

"My friend was completely blind and now he can see," came the reply.

Then the Holy Spirit said, "There is a person near you now who also needs healing in her eyes." I asked for the person to stand and a lady arose and said in English, "I need healing in my eyes."

"What is the matter?" I asked.

"I have been blind in one eye from birth," was her reply.

My faith almost failed me. The previous person had been completely blind, but I had not known that before I prayed. Sometimes there is nothing worse than knowing the exact condition of the person before you pray.

However, we do not operate in our own faith but in the faith the Lord gives us. I prayed a simple prayer and again this person fell on the ground.

A few moments later she stood up and shouted, "I can see perfectly!"

These healings caused people's faith to rise and miracle after miracle began to take place.

Suddenly the Holy Spirit said to me, "My power is falling on the right hand side of the meeting. Go over there."

I walked over to that part and hundreds began to fall under the power of the Spirit.

He then directed me to the middle of the gathering and I walked towards the middle of the crowd. Again hundreds fell under the power of the Spirit.

Finally He said, "My power is falling on the left hand side of the meeting," and as I walked over there the same thing happened.

About 1500 people came out after the message to receive Jesus Christ as Lord and Saviour. Again there was a mighty baptism of the Holy Spirit.

The next night was a repeat of the first.

The Holy Spirit, as usual, directed me to people for whom to pray and great miracles of healing took place.

Then, remarkably, the Holy Spirit said in the same way as the previous night, "My power is falling on the right hand side of the meeting."

I said this aloud and as I walked over to the right of the meeting about 150 people fell in a perfect circle.

Then the Holy Spirit said, "My power is falling in the centre of the gathering." So I walked to the centre and about 200 people fell in a perfect circle, with their feet facing the middle of the circle.

Then He said, "My power is falling on the left hand side of the meeting," and as I announced it I heard people falling everywhere and when I got over there, again they were in a perfect circle.

As I completed the altar call, a girl walked up to the platform. She could not speak English, but she was pointing at her ears. The power of God was so strong that I only had to say, "Be healed in the name of Jesus," and it happened.

This was some of the easiest healing I have ever experienced.

Later, as the power of the Holy Spirit fell, nearly 2000 were baptised in the Holy Spirit and spoke in tongues.

The Commissioner of Police said to me, "Do you realise, Bill, that out in that crowd there are some of my toughest cops? They have been weeping before God and now are praising God in tongues." Again, those seeking the baptism of the Spirit were transfixed for nearly an hour under the power of the Holy Spirit.

During the repentance call, Pat, who was seated some distance away, said to a friend, "That sounds like an aeroplane going over."

Her friend replied, "No, that is not an aeroplane, that is the crowd repenting."

Yes! People who have lived close to nature all their lives, such as the people of Papua New Guinea, are open to the power of God. They really repent and they have much to teach us.

Yes! Jesus did say, "These signs will follow those who believe." There is no doubt that when miracles occur there is an immediate response. Jesus preached with signs following and this is how He expects His disciples to preach.

Thousands followed Him as they saw these signs and He wants the same for us. The signs follow the believers, the believers do not follow the signs!

Each evening many testified concerning their healings. Some were doctors, others lawyers, others ordinary folk who had just attended the meetings. Some had been healed of asthma, crippling back conditions, lumps, eyesight problems

Papua New Guinea is an amazing country. Until a few years ago, it was administered by the Australians, and it is now independent. The nation proclaims itself Christian.

In the Highlands of Papua New Guinea, there have still been bow and arrow wars as recently as just a few years ago.

Cannibalism and tribal warfare was rampant throughout the country as recently as 50 years ago.

The first white settlers arrived about 120 years ago, though most of the country was largely uncivilised until recently. It has extremely steep terrain and some of the interior mountains rise as high as 5000 metres.

The principal transport is by air because of the rugged nature of the country. Many Christian missionaries operate in the area, relying principally on air transport.

In my Port Moresby meetings, while praying for a group of Christians, powerful demonic forces began to operate. The Holy Spirit led us to pray against various demons which named themselves, including cannibalism. The noise was so great and the manifestations so strong in the hotel room, that we thought all the staff and guests would be upset by the noise. Specific spirits of cannibalism manifested relating to desire for legs, arms and other parts of the anatomy and, after a hectic deliverance session, the people concerned were set free.

Another miracle to occur in Papua New Guinea involved a Lutheran pastor, Father van Bruggen. He had been a missionary in Papua New Guinea for 40 years, but felt he was coming to the end of his service.

However, after watching a film on renewal from Pastor Yonggi Cho's church in Korea, Father van Bruggen began to pray for renewal in his own church.

Then he visited England and was given a copy of my video, "Receiving the Gifts of the Holy Spirit." He took it back to his remote village in Papua New Guinea where, interestingly enough, he had a video player and the power to run it.

When he came to the part where I encouraged people to receive the baptism with the Holy Spirit, the power of God suddenly filled his room. He fell under the Holy Spirit and when he came to himself an hour later, the video player was still playing.

As he got up, he found he was speaking in tongues and when he walked among his people, the power of God fell on them and many were healed.

With this, revival broke out. About 1500 of his pupils were affected and they began to go and tell others in adjacent villages about the power of God.

The bishops in the Lutheran Church heard about this renewal and some were so perturbed about it that they decided to return Father van Bruggen to Holland.

Much prayer went up and the synod later reversed this decision.

One young man who was converted as a result of this move of the Spirit, became head of the young people's movement in the Lutheran Church in Papua New Guinea. He approached the bishops and asked whether I could speak at a major convention and, surprisingly, they agreed.

After receiving the invitation, I wrote back and set out exactly what I would do, namely preach on salvation, baptism with the Spirit, receiving the gifts of the Spirit and deliverance, including the casting out of demons. This programme was agreed to.

Pat and I flew to Port Moresby and from there we went to Lae and then to the Highlands. We were taken into an area so remote that the four-wheel drive vehicle could not get through the mud and we had to walk.

Preparations had been made over the previous six months for 4000 Lutherans from all over Papua New Guinea to be present. Crops had been grown and bush houses built.

We were led up to an old mission house above the village, noticing on the way that the high grass around the house had been cleared.

That night, while Pat was out the back of the house, Michael Roi, my host, told me they had cleared the ground because of the snakes. Pat had said she hated snakes so he did not want to tell her.

The mission was a great success. I spoke for three days and nights. The interpreter was a fine German Lutheran who had been born in Papua New Guinea and lived there all his life. He was conservative and not involved in charismatic renewal.

On the third day he broke down as the power of God fell on him, and, under the conviction of the Holy Spirit, began to give his testimony.

It astounds me how people who have only come into modern civilisation in the past two or three generations respond to the Gospel of Jesus Christ and to the gifts of the Holy Spirit. As I taught in the area of the gifts I saw many people come into the word of knowledge, gifts of healing and discernment of spirits, as well as other gifts.

At the end of the convention, thousands lined the roads and wept openly. In those few days God had bound us together in a mighty way in the Spirit with them.

As we proceeded towards the airport, Michael told me the rest of the mission house story.

Some days earlier, he had gone to the house and heard a noise in the roof. On investigation he found a 2 metre snake, then, under the front steps, he discovered a death adder. And, on the way to the toilet from the back door, he had come across a snake in the tree.

They had also cleared snakes from where I had been speaking, both under the platform and from the adjacent trees.

I pointed out that we had walked half an hour each day from the mission house through the long grass into the village and back again, both during the day and at 10 o'clock at night, and asked him what protection he thought we had.

He said he had believed the Lord would protect us. He truly did.

TWELVE

Poorest of the Poor

One day as I sat in my housing company office, I received a call from a competitor who asked me whether I knew Terry Calkin, the director of another building company. He pointed out that the views of Terry's directors did not coincide with our own view in regard to representations to the Government. In fact, in some ways they seemed to contradict our point of view.

He wondered what could be done about it because unless we presented a united front to the Government, there could be problems.

I didn't know Terry, but I made further enquiries and found out that he was, in fact, a Christian.

I called him one day, we talked, and I suggested that our boards came together for prayer. Although we were competitors at business, Terry agreed.

He and his board came to our office and we had a joint meeting and prayed for each other's business and for one another personally.

Out of this a lasting friendship developed. In fact, the two companies went into a joint venture to export houses to the Middle East.

Today Terry is pastor of one of the fastest-growing Pentecostal churches in Auckland. God gave him a vision to establish a church in a strategic position and that church is being used by the whole Body of Christ for various meetings. It is a real blessing.

Over the years, Terry and I have been able to encourage each other in various ways. Neither of us are in the building business any more, but we are now able to operate together in a far better business, namely the King's business.

Terry had a particularly effective ministry in India at the time I first met him. He had been there a number of times, leading teams and getting tremendous results in conjunction with his brother-in-law, Stuart Gramenz of Australia. Their International Outreach campaigns to India had caused thousands to turn to the Lord and they had established a Bible college in India.

At Terry's invitation, Pat and I agreed to take part in a crusade in the south Indian town of Gundar, about 500 kilometres north of Madras. We took John, our younger son, with us.

We flew into the heat of Madras and took a taxi to our hotel. Beggars were everywhere and the traffic was a nightmare. We flew in an ancient Air India aeroplane from Madras to a small airport about 100 kilometres from Gundar and then travelled in an elderly vehicle on to Gundar itself.

Gundar is a town of about 25,000 people. It is situated on a plain and in March you can almost cut the shimmering heat with a knife as the sun seems to stand motionless in the cloudless sky. Everything is hot and dusty.

We were booked into a place which was described as a hotel, but it proved to be a concrete building with very poor facilities. The stairwell stank of urine and excrement and the air conditioning was appalling.

Even outside we had to be careful where we walked because human excrement was everywhere. The stench was horrible.

In India the drinking water can be dynamite. It transmits all sorts of diseases and unless it is boiled you are in for major health problems. People draw water from wells around which they are urinating. Even in the hotel in Madras, we found that we became ill.

The only way Terry ensures his team members keep well is to put one of their staff in the hotel kitchen. He finds that the problem is that the Indians frequently do not boil the water in which they are washing the dishes, and this causes diseases to be easily transmitted.

I asked Terry how he went about conducting the crusades, and particularly how he went about healing. Quite airily he said to me, "Just take a leper, a deaf and dumb person and a blind person out of the crowd and pray for them. God will do the rest."

When I arrived the first night, about 9000 people had gathered.

A number of churches were supporting the crusade, which was held in an open field. A rough and ready stand had been erected. There were about 28 in the team.

To avoid people being injured in the crush during the prayer time after the meetings, fences like cattle races had been erected so those requiring prayer could form lines and be prayed for individually by team members.

The first night, as Terry suggested, I went into the crowd and, through an interpreter, asked for deaf and dumb children to come forward. About 60 appeared as though by magic in front of me. I went along the line and asked the

Lord to indicate one to me. At about the 10th He seemed to say to pray for that particular child. One of the pastors, who was also a doctor, checked out the child and ensured that he was, in fact, deaf and dumb.

I then asked for leprosy sufferers to come forward and about 100 appeared. Again I selected one after waiting on the Lord and my pastor friend stuck needles into his arms and hands to ensure there was no feeling. It was obvious that most of the people had leprosy because parts of their hands and fingers were missing.

Finally, I asked for the blind or near-blind to come forward and again there was a great crowd. Out of the line I selected a person who was almost totally blind. I told my three candidates for healing to sit on the ground in front of the platform and went to the stage to wait for the evening proceedings to start. The New Zealanders were seated behind me on the platform.

I preached my heart out that night, telling the crowd about the love of God, the cross of Jesus Christ and what it meant, and the need for repentance. From time to time I glanced down at the three seated in front of me. They were listening attentively.

The interpreter was doing an excellent job, copying almost every action. I preached longer than usual because, quite frankly, I was almost wishing the candidates for healing would go away.

However, when I could delay no longer, I asked for the deaf and dumb child to be brought on to the platform. He was about eight years of age. I told the crowd what I was about to do and that God would heal that child. As I began to pray for the child, I turned to my 28 compatriots on the platform and shouted, "Pray as hard as you can. Agree with me. Pray! Pray!"

Bill at seven years old.

Bill and Pat on their wedding day

The Subritzky family (left to right)
Paul, Janne, Bill, Pat, Maria and John.

Thousands gather at a World Vision camp in Ethiopia.

Bill *with* His Majesty King Taufa'ahau Tupou IV *of* Tonga
and Princess Siuilikutapu.

Bill *with the former* Prime Minister *of* New Zealand,
the Right Honourable Mike Moore.

Preaching in night meeting in Rabaul, Papua New Guinea.

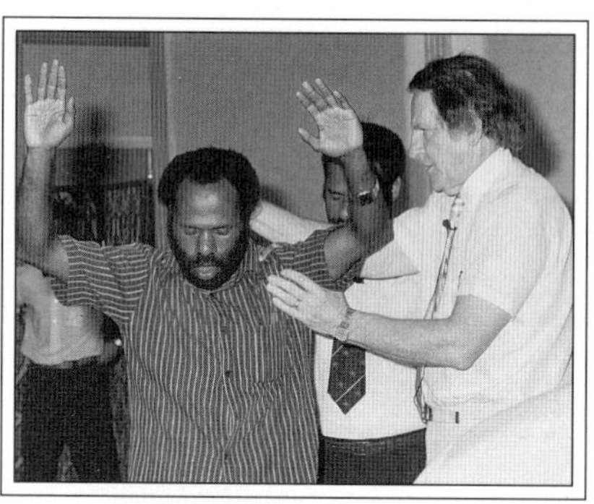

Praying for the sick in Papua New Guinea.

Bill with Dianne Parker and her son, Grant, miraculously healed from a crippling spinal disease.

The Dove

Addressing teenagers at Y.F.C. Summer Harvest Camp on Bill's farm in the Bay of Islands.

(Above and below): Bill *speaking at the* World Convention *of the* Full *Gospel* Business *Mens* Fellowship *International*, Detroit, USA.

*Praying for a delegate at the "*Battle Belongs *to the* Lord*"*
pastors and leaders conference, Brighton Centre, England.

Teaching with interpreter at a conference in Budapest, Hungary.

Bill and Pat teaching together on "Healing Marriages and Family Relationships" at the Greenlane Christian Centre, Auckland, New Zealand.

Bill and Pat Subritzky with their married sons, daughters, sons-in-law, daughters-in-law and grandchildren.

I then led the prayer for the young boy, after which my pastor friend spoke to him. To my amazement, the child answered. The power of God flooded the platform. The crowd shouted with joy.

That was one of them dealt with.

Now I called for the almost-blind person to be brought up. Again I shouted to the New Zealanders to pray with all their might and I sensed the anointing fall on the man. When I finished I told him, through the interpreter, to look to the back of the stadium and asked whether he could see any better.

One of the confusing habits which these people seem to have is that when they say "yes" they shake their heads and when they said "no" they nod.

Accordingly, when this person shook his head, I thought he meant no. It was only when I saw the excitement in the crowd that I realised that, in fact, the blindness had lifted from the person.

It was then the turn of the leprosy sufferer. He was helped to the platform and again I shouted to the New Zealanders to pray with all their might and to put their hands out towards me. With greater faith this time, I prayed. We felt the anointing of God falling on the man. When I had finished I found he was already moving his remaining fingers freely. My pastor friend pushed needles into his hands and arms and it was clear that he could now feel pain. The healing power of God had flooded his body. A great shout went up from the crowd.

Many came forward for salvation. The rest of the team went down and prayed for the sick until a late hour.

I followed the same procedure for several nights. Healings always occurred. God never failed.

Sometimes you have to be recklessly bold and step

out and believe God will do the rest.

On the final night, at the close of the meeting, I asked for those who had been healed to come forward. An enormous crowd began to pour forward and formed such a crush that the stand began to collapse. We rushed away, fearing injury, and made our way alongside the crowd and into the van which was to take us back to our "hotel".

When I returned to New Zealand, I went to see my bishop. It had been my practice to visit him once a year and tell him what was happening. He was a very kind and gracious man and very patient.

John had taken a video of the meetings and while the lighting was not excellent, it was still clear what had been happening. I showed one of the videos to the bishop, who watched with great interest as the sick, the blind, and the deaf and dumb were healed on the platform.

When the video was finished he simply said, "That must have been very tiring on you." There was no other comment.

I did not know whether he believed that the people had been healed or not, and went away humbled.

Most of my overseas trips have involved speaking at seminars or crusades.

However, my trip to Ethiopia in the mid 1980s was something very different — in more ways than one.

This trip came as a direct result of God speaking to me in my Bible reading. I have read my Bible daily ever since I was born again, realising early on in my walk with the Lord that Satan would put before me Scriptures which were out of context in order to confuse me.

If I did not know my Bible, I would have no way of responding.

I have divided my Bible into four sections — Genesis to

Job, Psalms to Malachi, the Gospels and Acts to Revelation. In this way it takes me about three months to read the Old Testament, 14 days to read the Gospels and 21 days to read Acts to Revelation. This gives me a balanced diet.

One morning, the Scriptures for the day included Matthew chapter 25. As I read from verse 31 onwards, the Lord began to speak to me about the hungry, the thirsty, the stranger, the naked, the sick and those in prison.

Jesus said in verse 40: "And the King will answer and say to them, 'Assuredly, I say to you, inasmuch as you did it to one of the least of these My brethren, you did it to Me.'"

As I read that Scripture, two messages came to my mind. One was "Ethiopia" and the other was "World Vision".

In those days a great famine was in progress in Ethiopia and harrowing scenes of terrible suffering were being shown nightly on our television screens.

However, I had only a limited knowledge of World Vision. I had sponsored a child for many years but knew little about the organisation itself.

I gave no further thought to this matter, but the next day the same messages kept coming into my mind. This happened continuously for 14 days and I began to realise God was speaking to me.

I have long since understood that God speaks to us by thought, impression, vision or audible voice.

Believing this could be of the Lord, I contacted Peter McNee, the director of World Vision in New Zealand, and he invited me in for lunch and showed me a further heart-rending video of Ethiopia.

As I said farewell to Peter, he turned and said, "Bill, unless you walk in the midst of that suffering, you will never understand it."

Over the next few weeks, I could not shake these words out of my mind. I did not want to go to Ethiopia under any circumstances, but finally recognised the Lord was speaking to me again.

So I called Peter and told him I was willing to go if he could get me into Ethiopia. He assured me he could and I arranged to meet him in Kenya about a month later.

I had to fly via Australia, Singapore and the Seychelles. As I disembarked from the plane in the Seychelles and went into the airport building, I noticed a woman passenger standing near me. She was quite an attractive woman in her early forties.

We completed entry formalities and as I was walking towards the exit area she approached me and said, "I believe you are staying in the same hotel as me." She had overheard me speaking to somebody else.

I confirmed this, and she suggested we got a taxi together. I saw nothing wrong with this, so we packed our bags into the car and went to the hotel.

It was about 11 o'clock in the morning and she suggested we had a drink together. I declined.

Then I went out on to a beautiful beach where I found Europeans walking naked. Apparently this was the place to come for nude swimming.

I went for a swim and was soon joined by this woman, who was starting to pester me.

That afternoon she again approached me to have a drink with her. Not wanting to appear rude, I reluctantly said yes. We sat on the terrace and I had an orange juice. She told me she worked for the United Nations and was going to Africa, where she was working on a project.

I was glad when the time came that night to go back to

the airport to catch our plane. But to my dismay, she was assigned a seat next to me and I could feel an almost overwhelming presence coming from her. I recognised it as lust.

She suggested that we see each other when we got to Kenya, but I told her quite bluntly that I was a Christian and I was not prepared to compromise my position.

At the airport in Nairobi, she asked if she could share my taxi. As I was going to the hotel where the World Vision workers were staying, I saw no problem with this and agreed to drop her off at her hotel.

In the taxi, she continued speaking about seeing me again and, as we arrived at her hotel, she suddenly turned to me and made a very enlightening observation, "Have you ever sensed that somebody is sitting beside you when, in fact, there is nobody there?"

I suddenly realised the whole of Satan's ploy. This woman had a demon with her which was attempting to trigger off a reaction within myself in her favour.

I was glad to say goodbye to her.

Peter McNee had already arrived in Nairobi, and we went to the Ethiopian embassy to get our visas. There were many people gathered around the embassy and we could not get any sense out of the person behind the counter. We went back the next day and the same thing happened. By the third day we realised we were not going to be granted a visa.

In the meantime, I had been invited to speak at the Nairobi Town Hall to a large meeting which takes place there each day. A number of people responded to the call.

After the meeting I prayed for some of the World Vision staff. The Lord gave me excellent words of knowledge concerning their circumstances. Some of them had considerable sin in their lives. As the Lord disclosed this and the circumstances, many were taken aback. I was speaking to them individually in a separate office, and as they left to go and get their spouses for further prayer, they reported what was happening.

Before long we had a great crowd gathered outside the offices, awaiting prayer. It was certainly a blessed time.

Finally, Peter and I decided it was no use waiting any longer, but that we should go direct to Addis Ababa, the capital of Ethiopia. If the Lord was with us, somehow we could get through customs.

As our plane landed, we could see World Vision staff waving our visas. God was indeed with us.

We drove into the dusty old capital and saw that many of the buildings had been torn down. In the centre of the town there was a large empty square. Since 1975 Ethiopia had been a communist country, although recently that government has been overturned.

There were not many people in the streets and those who were there looked thin and bedraggled. Communist slogans were everywhere.

As we drove up to our dilapidated hotel, we found about 500 young children standing in front of it, begging for food or money. What could one do in such circumstances? We had to make our way through the crowd and into the hotel.

As I sat down to a meagre meal, I felt guilty thinking of the children outside and the starvation taking place in the country.

We travelled from Addis Ababa to the first camp in a small plane owned by World Vision. As we crossed the countryside, I saw how accurate the Bible is when it speaks of the great ravines of Ethiopia. We flew over a large flat plain which looked brown and dusty, then over an enormous canyon, similar to the Grand Canyon in the United States. At the bottom we could see a trickle of water which was, in fact, a great river. Villages dotted the sides of the river. One wondered how the inhabitants ever contacted civilisation. Then we came to a mountain range, then a further plain and finally we were flying over some iron-roofed buildings. We circled and it seemed like thousands of black ants were gathered around, but as we lost altitude, I realised they were people.

We landed on the dirt airstrip and were escorted by soldiers through a squalid village towards the camp.

As we approached, I noticed many people turning towards us. Some were crawling, some were walking, some were limping, but all were screaming. There were maybe 100 or more, clad only in rags, their bones protruding through their skin.

It was my first meeting with starving people.

The next moment they simply overwhelmed us. Daylight disappeared until the guards rushed in to save us, dragging the people away.

As we made our way to the camp, the guards forcibly, rather brutally in fact, parted the crowd standing near the gates.

Inside the camp, I saw on the left-hand side World Vision staff sitting at a small table, measuring and weighing the people one by one and giving them such food as their body could manage.

Then we walked into a large building where at least 1000 women were breast-feeding their babies. I learned that the majority of them had walked over 150 kilometres to this camp. They had left their husbands in their villages, hoping for rain so they could plant crops.

A few wore Coptic Christian crosses, but at least 80 per cent were Muslim.

There was complete silence. Not a child was crying. A thousand sets of grateful eyes fastened on us, recognising us as people who had cared for them.

About 15 minutes later as we walked out into the sunshine, the words from Matthew chapter 25:40 came ringing in my ears: "And the King will answer and say to them, 'Assuredly, I say to you, inasmuch as you did it to one of the least of these My brethren, you did it to Me'."

I said, "Lord, most of those people in there were Muslim. Are You calling them Your brethren?"

As I began to ponder the Scripture, I realised that Jesus Christ came in the flesh, and that for the purpose of this Scripture He regards the poor, the sick, the hungry, the thirsty, the stranger, the naked and those in prison as His brethren. I know full well that unless we are born again of the Holy Spirit, we are not a son or daughter of God. But I believe that in this particular Scripture, Jesus is referring to these people in a special way as brethren. Jesus uses the word "brethren" in a number of Scriptures in a much wider context than we would usually understand it. For example, in Mark 3:35, He says: "For whoever does the will of God is My brother and My sister and mother."

He expected Bill Subritzky to have the same compassion for these six groups of people as He Himself had.

Suddenly I could see that, while Jesus did not want me to become ensnared in the affairs of this world, He did expect me to take care of this group of people. He brought me 18,000 kilometres to teach me this lesson.

People were dropping dead around us and they were taken on stretchers to an adjacent hill where thousands more were gathered.

We went up there to see another scene of terrible devastation. Here people who themselves were dying were burying their dead. They stripped the rags off the bodies and with their bare hands scraped graves about 2 metres deep out of the stones.

Then they placed the bodies in the graves, one on top of the other. People were reaching down to touch their dead and themselves falling into the grave. They were too weak to climb out and others had to drag them from the grave.

The screaming, screeching, weeping and grieving was unbearable. One could only stand and weep.

We spent that night in a small building adjacent to the camp, but I could not sleep.

In the early hours of the morning I heard a buzzing like bees. It was thousands of people stirring on the outside of camp. They had stayed there all night in the cold. In the day it was stifling hot but at night it was freezing.

At dawn the terrible screams began as people found their loved ones dead beside them. Somebody was finding a dead wife, or daughter, or mother, or father. Grief was overwhelming.

As we walked through the camp that day, we recognised that the only hope there was the Christian hope.

We asked many Muslims walking around the camp what they thought of the workers wearing the uniforms. Invariably the answer came back through the interpreter, "They are Christians."

We would then ask, "Why do you say they are

Christians?" and the answer came back, "Because they are helping us."

Suddenly I realised the wisdom of God. He knew 2000 years ago that the time would come in a place like Ethiopia where the Gospel could not be preached. At that time you would have been immediately imprisoned if you tried to share the Gospel.

Later, in Addis Ababa, I met a Pentecostal pastor who had been imprisoned for eight years for refusing to salute the communist flag. He told me there were 169 other pastors similarly imprisoned.

God knew the only way the Gospel could be preached in Ethiopia, and in many other countries, would be by showing the love of Jesus Christ. As this love was demonstrated, Muslim hearts were touched.

A lump came to our throats as we watched trucks coming over the horizon, carrying supplies into the camp. Many had been ambushed by terrorists, many had to go over a very rocky road. But some got through. We realised this was the lifeline for these people.

A government official told us that without help from World Vision, all these people would have died.

One day, as we walked around the outside of the camp, I saw people bending over and looking at the ground. They were picking up small seeds of wheat which had already passed through other people's bodies. They were so hungry that they would eat anything.

From there we flew to another camp, where we discovered why we had been obstructed from entering Ethiopia. This camp of 50,000 people had been beset by nine of the worst plagues known to mankind. The Government had decided that all these people should be sent home. Many refused, so they had been driven out at the point of the bayonet.

Thousands died on the roadside. The world media heard about it and trumpeted the whole affair, so the Ethiopian Government shut its borders while it sorted out the problem.

Now World Vision had become involved. It had set up a large camp of army tents on one side of the road, and on the other side about 40,000 people were gathered. Some were going up in the adjacent hills and picking small branches and twigs in order to make some covering for themselves.

The communist commander told us that as soon as people took ill in the camp, he sent them across the road to the World Vision camp. As we went through the hospital, we found 24 Australian and New Zealand doctors and nurses working under appalling circumstances. Sanitary conditions were horrible and the heat was unbearable, as were the flies and mosquitoes. However, these dedicated people were working with and ministering to hundreds of sick people as they lay on the ground with blankets over them. This thin line of 24 selfless workers stayed that plague and saved tens of thousands of lives. I often think that these people deserve honours from their country. However, I believe their names are written on a better honours board in heaven.

The communist commander took us into the centre of the grounds, where we were well clear of anybody, and suddenly broke into fluent English. He told us he had just been appointed to the camp and that he was a Christian.

Then we recognised how fortunate we were to live in a country with freedom of speech. This man was clearly afraid to tell everybody he was a Christian, because he would have been instantly dismissed and imprisoned. However, he gave us the freedom of the camp and we were able to travel around and photograph many of the scenes.

When we returned to Addis Ababa, I received a message to telephone New Zealand.

I called Pat and found out that our son, John, had been taken ill with peritonitis. His appendix had burst and he was in hospital. Pat said the doctors had told her they would not know for 24 hours whether he would live.

Now I was so glad I had not succumbed to the spirit of lust from that woman on the plane. It meant I could come to the Lord with clean hands.

As I prayed, the Lord gave me the Scripture from Deuteronomy chapter 33:26-27: "There is no one like the God of Jeshurun, Who rides the heavens to help you, and in His excellency on the clouds. The eternal God is your refuge, and underneath are the everlasting arms; He will thrust out the enemy from before you, and will say, 'Destroy!'"

I telephoned Pat to tell her that I had received this Scripture from the Lord. She had just received exactly the same Scripture and at the same time the Lord had given her a wonderful prophecy concerning John's future.

Needless to say, John fully recovered.

On our way home, we went through Bombay, India, where thousands of people live on the footpaths. They are born there, they die there.

One wonders how people can walk around them and take no notice. That is, of course, until one understands that Hindus believe in reincarnation and that they believe these people are paying the penalty for the sins of their past lives. I thank God that I do not have to die and come back as a bird, a dog, a horse or another person in order to pay for the sins of this life, but that Jesus Christ has done this for me on the cross.

However, the principal point is that I believe no other world "religion" has the compassion of God so clearly shown as it is in Christianity. No other religion has a Saviour sent by God, the Son of God Himself, to die on the cross for us. Therefore, I believe it behoves Christians to show much greater compassion, because we have the heart of God Himself with us.

Soon after my African experience, I went to Brazil to speak in a major conference.

While in Recife, I visited the slums. As we passed these houses of cardboard and corrugated iron, I noticed an occasional one that was nicely painted. It housed a family sponsored by World Vision. We reached the water's edge and clambered up a 2 metre ladder into a shack well above the water line. A Portuguese lady there greeted us effusively and pointed at a picture on the wall.

I looked at it and saw a New Zealand couple who were sponsoring this family, in which there were eight children without a father. The sponsors' money was all that prevented this woman and her family from starving.

In another part of the slum, I asked my World Vision hosts whether they prayed for the sick. They had never been taught that they could, so they were somewhat surprised.

They then suggested that I go into a round brick building which was partly sunken into the ground. They said there was somebody there for whom I should pray.

I walked down the steps, and as my eyes became accustomed to the darkness I saw the form of a woman crawling on her hands and knees. The stench was horrible. She had been crawling around in this manner for three years, living in her own excrement.

There was no escape. I had to pray for her. I laid hands on her in the name of Jesus Christ and commanded her to be healed. Fortunately she had a Catholic background and therefore believed in God.

Suddenly she stood erect, totally healed. She walked out of that building and her daughter-in-law fainted.

It was the first time for over three years that she had seen her mother-in-law walk.

Then they brought a deaf and dumb boy to me. As I laid hands on him, he was instantly healed. Within a few minutes we had a great procession of people following us. I was privileged to pray for many of them but, because I was scheduled to leave, I had to go back to the airport to catch a plane.

My main reason for being in Brazil was to speak at a Full Gospel Business Men's convention.

In the preliminary meeting I noticed that many Brazilian Pentecostals were upset because Full Gospel insisted that Catholics could join the organisation.

Many Full Gospel leaders from the United States testified how God had moved among the Catholics and how many Catholics were, in fact, members of the fellowship. However, they did not seem to be able to persuade their Brazilian hosts, who seemed hostile to the Catholic Church.

On the night it was my turn to speak at the convention, I gave my testimony and, in the course of it, began to speak about God's move among the Catholics, pointing out that about 80 million Catholics around the world had been baptised with the Holy Spirit and spoke in tongues.

Suddenly there was a disturbance in the centre of the auditorium and a man began to shout. I thought he was bringing a message in tongues so I waited for him. Then my interpreter said, "No, the man is very upset." Soon he had about 50 people around him and they were making a loud noise.

I called on the singers to lead us in the song, "He is Lord". This quietened the gathering. Then I spoke again about what God was doing among the Catholics. Again the same shouting erupted, but this time more violently. Again we led in worship and the meeting became quiet. I began to speak again, but by now people were becoming very angry. Some of those on the floor were beginning to shake their fists. Paul was with me on that trip and he came to me and said, "Dad, you had better get out of the place. There is going to be a riot."

However, I persisted. I told the people they should repent of their attitude and waited for the conviction of the Holy Spirit to fall. Finally I sensed a change coming over the crowd. In the end nearly 1000 of the crowd of 2000 came forward and fell on their knees and repented of their attitude towards the Catholics.

My experiences with World Vision in Ethiopia and Brazil were the start of a long and fruitful ministry with the Christian aid organisation.

I rejoiced that God had moved in such a way.

Two years later I went to Thailand to observe the work of World Vision there and in the great slum area of Bangkok, in which one million people reside, I was privileged to see large numbers of homes nicely painted and cleaned. Now World Vision was working with the whole community instead of individual families only. In many of these homes there were young women who had been prostitutes or on drugs and were now totally set free.

We then went to the rubbish tips of Bangkok, some of which were up to several hundred metres long and at least 30 metres high. On top of them, we saw cardboard shacks inhabited by squatters who scrabbled among the rubbish and rats to find plastic which they washed, placed in heaps and sold to the merchants in Bangkok for a few cents. Working among these people were young World Vision workers, who helped them and showed them the love of Jesus Christ. This is real dedication.

Many people say to me, "Why should we help people in countries where their governments are fighting wars, or where the rich should be looking after their own people?"

My response is that the Scripture in Matthew 25:31 and following says that Jesus Christ will one day sit on the throne of His glory and all the peoples will be gathered together and they will be separated as a shepherd divides his sheep from the goats. Each person, whether he is the ruler of a country or a private citizen, will be required to stand before God and give an account of his response to the hungry, the thirsty, the stranger, the naked, the sick and those in prison. Jesus describes these, for the purpose of this Scripture, as His brethren. I would not like to be in the shoes of a ruler of Ethiopia who waged a war instead of helping his poor, or a rich person in Brazil who ignored the poor around him. I frequently remind my audiences that, compared with a beggar living on the footpath in Calcutta, every person in New Zealand is a millionaire.

After returning from Ethiopia, I went to a Full Gospel Business Men's Fellowship convention in Wellington. I told them what had happened in Ethiopia and as I watched I noticed the Holy Spirit fall on them like wind on a wheat field. Dozens of them went down under the power of the Spirit.

Since my visit to Ethiopia, the Lord has impressed on me the need to help these people. Not long after I returned, He gave me a number of children to sponsor. At first I could not believe it was from the Lord because the number seemed too great. However, after further prayer, it was clear that I should support them.

Nowadays, in all my evangelistic outreaches, I press the case of the poor. In addition, I have found that the numbers of people responding to the Gospel have greatly increased. There is no doubt that when we preach the full Gospel of Jesus Christ and act on it, God moves in the hearts of people.

There was an interesting sideline to all this. I asked World Vision to send a representative to each of my meetings, but the man took ill and another man, Gordon Miller, replaced him.

Before Gordon went to work for World Vision, he had been a Presbyterian minister and had attended several of my public meetings. Following these, he would preach in his pulpit the next Sunday morning and criticise everything I did.

Now he was working for World Vision and was required to be in my meetings. I really believe the Lord has a sense of humour.

Gordon had to wait until the end of the meetings so people could sponsor children. As he listened afresh to my messages, God changed him from being antagonistic to being totally supportive. It is marvellous how God works.

As a result of our joint ministry, thousands of children have been sponsored.

Gordon has given me a letter, setting out his testimony in this area, and told me to freely use it with any clergy wherever I travel.

THIRTEEN

Politicians and Royalty

My early fervour to be involved in politics died a natural death while I was still a young man — firstly because I wanted to make money, and secondly because of my calling to preach the Gospel.

However, I have had regular involvement with politics and politicians over the years, including a number of Prime Ministers and other national leaders.

My involvement with Norman Kirk was cut short when he died in 1974.

A few years later, however, I met another prominent Labour politician, Mike Moore.

Mike had entered politics in 1972 at the age of 23 and had been an up-and-coming star. However in 1975, following a particularly antagonistic campaign, he had lost his seat.

He was devastated, and this was exacerbated when it seemed that nobody wanted to employ him. Finally he worked as a nurse in a psychiatric hospital while he contemplated his comeback into politics. In due course, in 1978, he won re-election.

I had known Mike for a number of years and wasn't surprised when he visited me just after the election.

I was surprised, however, when he began to unburden himself.

"I have melanoma and the doctors have given me three months to live," he told me.

Although he didn't say it, I knew Mike had come to seek help and I told him that I knew Jesus Christ could help him and prayed for him there and then.

He asked whether he should go to chemotherapy the following week and as I felt it was not my place to tell him he shouldn't I told him to go ahead.

During the next few months I visited him on a number of occasions, and prayed with him each time. The Rev James Worsfold, head of the Apostolic Church in New Zealand, came with me sometimes and we prayed together for Mike.

I was delighted to learn that his wife had been born again and baptised with the Spirit in the early 70s in a meeting conducted by Harry Greenwood. She was obviously very open to things of the Spirit and agreed with us in prayer.

Mike lost all his hair and became very ill, but he responded very well to prayer. Gradually he began to recover and finally, after about a year, appeared fully recovered.

"I am going back into Parliament to make my Lazarus speech," he told me.

In due course he reappeared in Parliament and was congratulated on all sides for his recovery. Mike makes reference to my visits to him during his illness in his book, "Hard Labour".

When the next Labour Government was elected, in 1984, Mike became the third-ranking minister as Minister of Overseas Trade. He travelled widely, promoting the interests of New Zealand.

In August 1990, I was conducting crusades in Japan. One day when I returned to my hotel, there was a message that the Prime Minister of New Zealand had tried to ring me and wanted me to call him back.

When I called, Mike Moore said, "Bill, well I have made it. I am Prime Minister."

Looking back on the 11 years since we had prayed for him, it was clearly a miracle. Despite the fact that his party was defeated at the 1990 elections, I believe God has many things yet in store for Mike Moore and his dear wife.

Another New Zealand Prime Minister I had an acquaintance with was David Lange.

Mr Lange claimed a Christian experience and was an admirer of the well-known English preacher, Lord Soper.

Before becoming Prime Minister, he had undergone an operation on his stomach and prior to the operation he asked me for prayer, which I gladly gave.

We were not close friends, but I rejoiced to see him become Prime Minister as I believed he would give good Christian leadership to the land.

To my dismay, and that of many other Christians, his Government decided to introduce a bill legalising homosexuality for people over 16. About a million of New Zealand's 3 million people signed a petition against this, yet the legislation proceeded through Parliament anyway.

As this happened, I wrote to Mr Lange and told him he had brought a curse on the land because, as a Christian, he had disobeyed a basic principle of God's Word. God treats homosexuality as an abomination, even though He forgives the homosexual as he turns to Him.

I had been convinced of this evil all my life, particularly in the light of the homosexual advances made to me as a boy and as a young man in the freezing works.

I didn't receive any reply from Mr Lange.

On October 18, 1987, during my annual holiday in Fiji, the audible voice of the Lord spoke to me, "The American stock market will drop 500 points and New Zealand will be under a curse for a further three and a half years."

I immediately rang my son, Paul, and told him what I believed I had received from the Lord.

That night the American stock market did fall 500 points and there was great panic. I subsequently realised God had given me an early confirmation of the first prophecy in order to show that the second was, in fact, true.

The Lange Government began to go into disarray. David Lange disagreed with his Minister of Finance and soon they were engaged in an unseemly public dispute.

I met another prominent politician and friend, Richard Prebble, on an aeroplane one day as we travelled back to New Zealand and told him of the letter I had written to Mr Lange.

He began to recount the events since August 1986 and said the seeds of the Government's destruction had clearly begun then.

Subsequently, Mr Lange's marriage failed and his Government fell to pieces and was routed in the elections in October 1990.

The three and a half years ended on April 19, 1991.

In the meantime, I told many people in my meetings up and down New Zealand of the curse which I believed had come on the land as the result of the homosexual bill. Unemployment had grown to nearly 10 per cent of the population, and in some parts of New Zealand was far worse. The country was under great depression.

It is noteworthy that in the week ended April 19, 1991, the country began a major economic turn-round. Inflation fell to almost nothing, interest rates dropped and the following month businessmen reported the greatest confidence they had had in decades.

Some say that economic events and spiritual events are often closely linked. I believe as New Zealand recovers from its recession, so indeed there will be a spiritual renewal.

I have over the years met many overseas politicians and leaders and also had considerable involvement with the Tongan royal family.

The nation of Tonga, consisting of about 100,000 people, is a beautiful cluster of small islands in the South Pacific.

It is unusual because it has a king who can trace his ancestry back at least 1000 years. He exercises great power, because the constitution puts most of the authority in his hands, together with the nobles, although there are some commoners in the parliament.

In the early 1970s God began to move in Tonga, during which time the Prime Minister, who was also Prince Regent, HRH Prince Fatafehi Tu'ipelehake, the King's brother, and his wife, HRH Princess Melenaite Tu'ipelehake, were both taking a great interest in Christian matters. From 1979 onwards Pat and I made many visits to Tonga for crusades. One night His Majesty King Taufa'ahau Tupou IV attended a meeting and the people watched with great interest because if he did not like anything he would simply walk out with his staff. However, he stayed for the full crusade so he must have appreciated the message.

On the first occasion Pat and I went to Tonga, the Prime Minister met me in an unusual way. I found that there was provision for me to meet him as he was acting as Prince Regent, on behalf of the King, His Majesty King Taufa'ahau Tupou IV, who was overseas.

I was told the Prime Minister would visit us at the hotel at 7.30pm one night.

As we waited for him to arrive, I heard sirens screaming. Next, a procession of military vehicles and troops stopped at the front door of the hotel and all the staff stood to attention while the Prime Minister walked in, followed by his officers.

He greeted Pat and me, then went to a small room and we were invited in.

As we sat and talked it was clear the Prime Minister wanted something. I soon realised he needed to be born again and baptised with the Holy Spirit.

He agreed for me to pray for him. He made his total commitment to Jesus Christ, was born again and came into the gift of tongues.

After a short conversation, he stood up and, having farewelled us, walked out of the hotel with his officers. He entered his car and, escorted by the troops and with sirens screaming, went on his way.

It was the first time I had ever seen anybody come escorted by troops to receive the baptism with the Holy Spirit. However, the ways of God are beyond our ways.

At a later meeting in a hotel in the main town of Nuku'alofa, the Holy Spirit gave me a clear word that there was a person in the crowd who had a leg 17 centimetres shorter than the other. The man who responded came forward on crutches, and I could clearly see that he had homosexual tendencies.

I asked how long one leg had been shorter than the other. He said, "Seven years."

Then I asked him how long he had been a homosexual. He said, "Seven years."

I told him that if he would renounce homosexuality he would be healed. As he did so and confessed Jesus Christ as his Lord, the shortened leg came down to full length and he walked away, healed.

The Prime Minister saw the man's friends were still standing around the door waiting to take him home. He therefore took him into his home for two years and ministered to him.

During one of their periodic visits to New Zealand, the King, His Majesty, King Taufa'ahau Tupou IV and the Queen, Her Majesty Queen Halaevalu Mata'aho, of Tonga asked us to visit them. The King wished to be baptised with the Holy Spirit, so I laid hands on him and he came into the gift of tongues. No Tongan subject could have laid hands on the King, but it was in order for a person such as myself to do so. Shortly afterwards Pat prayed for the Queen and she also came into the baptism with the Holy Spirit.

In 1985 the King made a statement at the Free Wesleyan Church (of Tonga) Conference, which was released by newspapers and Radio Tonga, to the nation. He said that everybody in Tonga needed to be born again and baptised with the Holy Spirit and speak in tongues.

The dominant denomination in Tonga is Methodist, the fruit of missionaries who went there in the late 1700s. The first group of 10 of them were massacred in 1797. They had been sent out by the London Missionary Society.

Subsequently, further missionaries followed and most of the kingdom was converted to Methodism, although there are some Anglicans and Catholics.

The people observe their Christian beliefs very strictly and no non-Christian event is permitted on Sundays. Of course, this can be rather legalistic if there is not a real moving of the Holy Spirit.

When I was in Tonga in 1985, the King told church leaders to hold a Holy Spirit seminar for all the Free Wesleyan Church of Tonga ministers and stewards in order to hear me speak about the baptism with the Spirit.

I did so and at the end of the day, in company with several others, prayed for all the ministers. Many of them had needed to be born again of the Spirit of God and we led them into true repentance and salvation. Then we prayed for the baptism with the Holy Spirit and all but one received it.

I have no doubt that the effect of this experience was very great in their subsequent ministry and in the history of Tonga.

My most recent visit to Tonga, late in 1992, was the start of one of the most productive periods of ministry I have ever experienced.

We were invited by the Tonga for Christ Ministries which had representatives from the Catholic Pentecostals, the Anglicans, the Methodist Church, The Assemblies of God, the New Life Church, the Tongan Fellowship for Revival, the Tongan Constitutional Church and the Salvation Army.

The crusade meetings were held in an enclosed stadium over three nights and a total of 18,000 people attended. At least 6500 came forward either for first-time commitments or recommitments to Jesus Christ.

His Majesty, King Taufa'ahau Tupou IV, and former Primer Minister, HRH Prince Fatafehi Tu'ipelehake, attended on each of the three nights, while Her Majesty,

Queen Halaevalu Mata'aho and the current Prime Minister, Baron Vaea, attended one night each. Many nobles and members of Parliament also attended, and some committed their lives to Christ.

The Lord was gracious in granting spectacular words of knowledge, and during the crusade many of the blind, the deaf, the dumb and the crippled were clearly healed. It was such a powerful demonstration of God at work that on the second night a prominent doctor, having seen the major healing miracles, rushed forward at the altar call and committed his life to Christ.

The meetings were broadcast on the national radio of Tonga, and were also videoed and shown on national television on the next three Sunday nights.

As the crusade began, I felt the Holy Spirit say to me that as I walked through the crowds people would be healed. I pondered on this, and realised it would be similar to what had happened in Acts 3 with Peter and John as the crippled man was healed, and Acts 5 as the apostles walked in Jerusalem and sick people tried to get into the shadow of Peter to receive healing. I also remembered Peter healing Aeneas and Paul healing a cripple at Lystra (Acts 14:9-10).

I believe the Bible is alive and relevant for today, and the miracles God did in Biblical times He can do again today. And this is exactly what happened to me in Tonga! As I walked through the people, hundreds stood and shouted that they had been healed. It was absolutely incredible.

Not that the healing was confined to people with whom I had contact. Several people were healed while they listened to the radio broadcasts. One woman flew from an outer island specifically to testify of healing in her legs and eyes.

Between crusade meetings, the Holy Spirit seemed to encourage me to go to the hospital in Tonga, and while there I visited a small ward where there was a young man who had been totally paralysed in a football accident. He could not even move his head.

The Holy Spirit indicated that I should not lay hands on him, just stand beside him, and as I did so the power of God vibrated through his body and he began to raise his legs and arms.

Nurses became hysterical and as a crowd began to gather the healing power spread to them as well — a man crippled in one leg was healed instantly and a tumour disappeared from another woman's stomach.

Meanwhile, God was still working in the body of the paralysed man. I waited with him for 30 minutes as he continued to vibrate, and by the time I left he was moving freely in every part of his body.

Pat and I then flew on to Western Samoa, again at the invitation of the National Council of Churches, and over 150 churches, from Catholic to Pentecostal, got behind the meetings.

During the three night meetings, about 35,000 people attended, with 25,000 coming forward and giving their lives to Christ for the first time or making recommitments. We had been asked to take 10,000 commitment forms to Western Samoa and most of them were used up at the opening meeting.

On the first night, the Lord showed me that the main healings would be among the blind, and several totally blind people were healed before the cameras.

On the second night, He said the deaf would be healed, and totally deaf people came forward and testified that they could now hear.

On the third night, He said it would be backs and people who had been crippled were able to walk and run around the grounds.

In addition, thousands more raised their hands claiming they had specific, clear healings.

The Prime Minister of Western Samoa attended the meetings and made a public commitment to the Lord, coming forward and kneeling on the ground with thousands of others. Some of his cabinet ministers were present, one of whom told me he had come the second night because his eyes had been healed the first night.

During our time in Western Samoa, I was taken to a small island where about 2000 people crowded into a hall, and in the space of three minutes, eight blind people were totally healed.

In both Tonga and Western Samoa, about 25 per cent of the population attended the meetings and 80 per cent of these gave their lives to the Lord publicly.

Pat and I have no doubt that one of the major contributing factors to the success of the crusades has been the intercession that has preceded them. We now have several hundred intercessors from a number of countries praying for the meetings and believe the Lord will raise up many more. Immediately before all crusades, major intercession meetings and prayer and fasting were held by the local people.

The result was an incredible presence of the Holy Spirit. Indeed in Western Samoa, many of the crowd, including unbelievers, claimed they could see a dove hovering above the stadium during the meetings.

FOURTEEN

Trials and Triumph

My Christian principles always meant I took stringent precautions to ensure all my business practices were above board. I was therefore rather shocked one day to receive a disturbing letter from the director of the Housing Corporation in Auckland, alleging that my housing company was encouraging people to make false declarations about the amount of deposit they held when they applied for a housing loan.

The corporation required each applicant to provide at least a 10 per cent deposit towards a new home. While it could be argued that home-buyers should have their full deposit at the time of the loan application, many were in fact saving so it would be available when their house was finished. Doubt existed whether the people should have the deposit at the time of application or at the time their loan was uplifted, sometimes months later.

I immediately talked to the local manager of the corporation and suggested a new system whereby we would disclose exactly what cash the person held at the time of the loan application and institute a savings scheme so that by the time the loan was uplifted our solicitors could certify that the full deposit was held.

This satisfied the corporation, and a great expansion of

our sales occurred because we were now able to offer a clear savings scheme to our clients.

Little did I know that the Lord was preparing me for an unexpected attack from the enemy.

At that time I was completing my book, "Demons Defeated" and visiting the United States to speak at a Full Gospel Business Men's conference in Seattle.

When my son, Paul, and his wife, Lynette, picked me up at the airport on my return, I felt something was wrong, although they said nothing.

On the way home, Paul said the Housing Corporation had discovered that many wage certificates filed with loan applications on behalf of our clients had been falsified. There appeared to have been a ring of people within our sales force who were using a false stamp to certify the earnings of the home-buyers.

When I went to my office that day I found that, indeed, several of the salespeople had been using a false stamp on wage certificates. By using this stamp, they had been able to certify that the client's wages had been within the requirements of the Housing Corporation and Social Security Department, and in that way housing loans had been granted. I did not know the extent of the fraud, but obviously the deeper it went the more the ramifications for our company.

The stamp was now held in custody by our managing director, along with a few other things belonging to some of the salespeople concerned.

During the next few days, as we investigated the position, we decided to give back to the salespeople any items belonging to them. In the process, a misunderstanding occurred and the stamp which had been used for fraudulent purposes was handed back to the person who had first used it.

The Housing Corporation, meanwhile, had put the matter in the hands of the police.

A Christian detective visited me, and over lunch we shared many of our beliefs and I prayed briefly with him. I told him we would open everything to the police and give them the utmost in co-operation, as we had tried to maintain our business in an open manner, with total honesty and integrity.

He appeared satisfied with this. Then his co-detective also visited me and I went over the same ground with him.

I told them that the following week I was due in the United States to speak at the world convention of the Full Gospel Business Men's Fellowship, but .promised them, however, that the officers of the company would help them in every way possible.

This visit to the United States was, in itself, a miracle. The previous year I had been invited to speak at a Full Gospel Business Men's convention in Sydney. After I had spoken, a director from the Full Gospel Business Men's Fellowship of the United States asked me whether I would speak in the next world convention.

Taken aback, I said I would pray about it and advise him within about a month. He, in turn, was surprised because he had expected me to readily agree to such a wonderful offer.

In due course I let him know I was prepared to come and so I was billed as a speaker at the 1980 world convention in Anaheim, California.

When I arrived I discovered that my co-speakers were men with household names — Oral Roberts and Pat Robertson.

Each of us was given a one-night slot and for the first time, the three major Christian television networks had combined to beam the proceedings of the convention throughout the United States and parts of Canada.

When the night came for me to speak, I felt the Lord give me a wonderful anointing. After I gave my testimony, I asked my family to come forward, as the Lord had told me to centre on them. In today's world the family is the major area of attack by the enemy.

As they came forward, the crowd burst into rapturous applause. Demos Shakarian, president of Full Gospel Business Men's Fellowship, wept as he watched.

That night, many within the convention made a decision for the Lord. The large bank of telephones operated by sponsors of the convention rang continuously over the next few days. Many Christian networks repeated the testimony day after day.

When I walked off the platform that night, I received a message from my managing director in New Zealand.

When I called him I found, to my dismay, that the police had raided our company. Forty policeman had come and taken all our relevant records. Worse still, they had brought with them the television cameras, and on the major television network throughout New Zealand that night it had been proclaimed that my company was involved in fraud.

The man in charge of the investigation had stood in the middle of our company offices and openly proclaimed that by the time the police had finished their investigation, the company would not exist. They were there to destroy the company.

They seized 750 files but interestingly enough, they only went back to the date after which every declaration had been completed with meticulous accuracy in order to satisfy the Housing Corporation. This had considerable implications later in the investigation.

I knew this was a major attack of the enemy. The two detectives had promised that the enquiry would go in a normal fashion and I had never expected them to act in this manner.

Demos Shakarian and several of the directors of Full Gospel Business Men's Fellowship prayed for me. The word that was given to me that night was from Isaiah 54:17: "'No weapon formed against you shall prosper, and every tongue which rises against you in judgment you shall condemn. This is the heritage of the servants of the Lord, and their righteousness is from Me,' says the Lord."

In addition, Pat had a word of great encouragement from the Lord that night: "'This is but a small thing,' says the Lord. 'I will protect you.'"

There was no alternative but for me to return immediately to New Zealand. It was Friday night and the next available plane was on Monday morning.

I prayed throughout the weekend and on the Monday morning, when I telephoned my office from Los Angeles, I was told the police had individually interviewed four of our secretaries and told them they were liable for seven years' imprisonment. They were also accused of having sex with me and the other executives of the company.

When I learned this, I contacted one of my legal partners, Terry Way, and asked him to get hold of the women concerned and draw up affidavits about their treatment.

We arrived back in New Zealand at 6am on the Tuesday, and as we went through customs two police officers came to meet me. They took me to a side room and began to interview me. I pointed out we had been travelling all night and I was not in the best frame of mind, but this made no difference and they insisted on carrying on the interview. It was clear that their major objective was to implicate me.

In the course of the discussion, they said our sales manager had been implicated because some of the salesmen had confirmed that he, too, knew about the fraud. I told them I did not believe them.

Finally I said I would meet them in the office that afternoon at 2pm.

In the meantime, I discovered that the stamp, which was some of the prime evidence, had been passed back to the chief perpetrator of the fraud. Naturally I was greatly concerned because it could appear that I had sought to hide the evidence.

I prayed about it, and as soon as the detectives came into the office that afternoon I told them what had happened. This appeared to satisfy them.

Then I pointed out that I did not like the way in which they were conducting the case. I felt it had been unfair of them to wait until I went overseas before raiding the company and bringing in the television cameras.

I then produced the four affidavits, signed by the young ladies they had interviewed. These set out the conduct of the police and the allegations and threats made against these women.

The officers were clearly taken aback. Only the previous day there had been a major report on police conduct in another case where a man had been wrongly convicted of murder and had served 10 years of his sentence. The Government had decided to release the man and the police were shown up in a very unfavourable light.

I told the detectives that unless they went on television that night and confirmed that the company was not involved in this fraud, I would take those affidavits to the television stations and have them read out.

The detectives agreed to issue a statement to this effect and the retraction was broadcast on the major television network that night and, with some difficulty, in the newspapers as well.

Knowing, however, that the newspapers and television stations would seek every avenue to attack the company and myself, and also that the police would continue to issue unsourced statements, I decided to take further action.

The newspapers had also alleged that the company had been engaged in fraud and clearly there was a basis for defamation action. I arranged for our legal office to write a letter to all the newspapers which had published the story, along with the television and radio stations, and tell them we were going to sue them for $10 million each. I knew that in some way I had to stop the media from acting like mad dogs.

The next day I was contacted by Richard Prebble, the Labour Opposition Member of Parliament for Auckland Central. He wanted to know what was going on, because when the news broadcast appeared on the television sets in the parliamentary restaurant, a leading member of the Government had stood up and said, "Now we have got him. We have got him at last." He was clearly referring to me.

I told Richard I did not understand what the man meant.

Interestingly, one of the main supporters in my prayer meeting had been the political organiser for the MP who had made the accusation. We had been in the habit of praying for him in our early morning prayer meetings for at least a year.

I went to my friend and showed him a letter Richard Prebble had written me about the matter. He was astonished, and wrote to his MP friend.

The letter that came back was equally astonishing. The MP had never met me, but he made some wild allegations along the lines that I used to lend money at high interest rates to people and sell up their homes. In addition, he said I owned a large yacht and when I came into a bay, I would anchor away from the other boats and would not be involved with them. Little did he realise, of course, that with a larger yacht, one has to give oneself plenty of room. It was not on account of snobbery that I didn't anchor closer to the others.

It was clear that demonic forces of jealousy had affected this man, and equally clear that other forces were at work against me. I knew in my heart that the battle had only begun.

The men in charge of the fraud squad were determined to promote their careers, and one of the ways of doing so would be to catch a "big fish" like me.

They began to interview every person who had purchased a home from us and, consequently, had signed a declaration to the Housing Corporation at the time of purchase. As there were two parties involved in each purchase, they were interviewing 1500 people.

On the following Saturday morning, I placed a half-page newspaper advertisement thanking everybody who was supporting the company in our time of trial. Many people rang me to say this was a master-stroke.

Not unreasonably, the banks and other authorities lending to our company, were concerned about the case. I immediately spoke to their managements and explained our side of the story.

The thing which worried me most of all, however, was that I did not know the depth of the problem. How many homes were sold subject to this problem? Obviously it affected our whole future because we always pre-sold our homes.

We conducted our own full enquiry, which was rather difficult without the files that had been seized by the police. We found that there were about 70 cases involved and revealed all of these to the police and lending authorities.

As the enquiry took its course, I was told there was a room at the police station bulging with files on our case. It was the largest enquiry of its nature for many years.

Not only were the 1500 people who had signed declarations interviewed, but their employers were also contacted. Each employer and person was asked what they thought of Bill Subritzky and the company.

The pressure on me was intense. Our monthly healing meetings were suspended because I could not cope with both the pressures of business and these meetings. Some Christians wrongly construed this as an admission of guilt.

The months passed.

During the probe, there was a major homicide which required many of the police to change enquiries. I thought the heat was coming off, but immediately after the investigation the police were back in force.

Many times when I walked up the road towards my company offices, my heart would sink as I saw another police car sitting outside.

The two police officers in charge of the investigation warned me that if I intervened in any way with their enquiries they would arrest me. I was not allowed to warn any of the staff concerning their legal rights.

The officers concerned would come into our offices, wander around and intimidate staff. The effect on morale was unbelievably bad.

Each day I would call a meeting of the remaining salespeople, as we had dismissed those who were clearly involved. Some of those who may have been involved were not dismissed because of the lack of evidence.

I did my best to keep up the morale. We had new sales promotions and carried on as though nothing had happened.

Interestingly enough, although the whole enquiry occupied our thoughts daily, we found that many members of the public were unaware of the events and continued to buy our homes. Of course, much prayer went up during all of this trial.

One day, one of our salesmen who was innocent of any involvement, was accused by the police of having falsified a declaration. The declaration had been taken before the clients' own solicitors and the salesman was not involved with it.

Fortunately, he contacted his lawyer who prevented the arrest. However, he was terrified.

For several months I would find him on the floor as I came to my office each morning. He was obviously drinking too much. Finally his wife left him and he became almost suicidal. I did my best to hold him together during the enquiry as I knew he was innocent.

When I enquired concerning the allegations that the company sales manager was involved, I found that this also was a false accusation. The two police officers had gone in mufti to the local hotel where several of the salesmen went for a drink after work. The officers had befriended some of the new salesmen and made such a comment as, "Don't you think (the sales manager) must have known about this fraud?"

One of these salesmen had said, "Yes, he must have known."

During this time, one of our staff involved in answering the sales enquiries was found to be unsatisfactory in her employment. She was dismissed.

Immediately she wrote to the police, alleging my complicity in the whole fraud. She claimed she had heard me talk about it, and even sent me a copy of her letter.

Fortunately there was no evidence to support her comments and the police had to ignore the letter. I followed the Biblical injunction of praying for a blessing on her.

Just before the trial, I received another blow. The Housing Corporation rang to say it was suspending payments on all loans. This would bankrupt us.

I immediately contacted the head office of the corporation and pointed out that this was totally unfair. We had disclosed the loans which we had found to be obtained on a false basis and they had no right to refuse to pay out on other loans. Fortunately, the decision was reversed.

Then the Christian detective came to see me on his own. As we talked, I turned on him and said, "Do you realise you are touching God's anointed and that you will suffer the consequences? You are falsely accusing me and trying to get me implicated in this whole case and you know that I am not guilty."

He stared at me, rather shocked.

The case was approaching a climax. Months had gone by and hundreds of enquiries had been made by the police.

One morning I was awakened at 6 o'clock by our managing director, who said the police had arrived at the homes of 35 of our staff and told them that they must go to the police station or be arrested. All of them were now being required to give statements.

I went to the office. The first of those arrested arrived back about 9am. They showed me a list of 50 questions they had been asked. The police had told them that if they lied on any of these questions they would be liable for seven years' jail. The last three questions implicated me. The police had said that if the person being questioned would implicate Bill Subritzky, then they would escape all penalties. I knew this was their final throw of the dice.

I sat all day on my chair and prayed. As the staff returned I questioned them and found that each one had refused to implicate me. Finally, at 4pm, the last of those involved returned to the office.

Even those whom I thought may have succumbed to the pressure had not done so. Again the police had failed in their attempt to implicate me.

By now it was November and the trial of the salespeople was due. The police were claiming that each of them would get at least seven years.

The first person to come before the magistrate was a young lady in her 20s who had been employed by us a year earlier. She was dressed very smartly.

The magistrate was an older man and obviously felt she should be treated with mercy and fined her $90. The police were hopping mad. This would set the pattern for the rest of the salespeople. The other four came up in due course and pleaded guilty. They were each fined $90.

The only ill effect for us was the fact that each of their

lawyers alleged that the company had pressed them into taking these fraudulent actions. However, under New Zealand law there is no way an offended third party, who is not an immediate party to the proceedings, can stand up in the court and state their case. Accordingly, we could do nothing about it.

I went to see the proprietor of one of the newspapers to ask him to give our side of the story but he refused to do so. We just had to put up with it.

When the trials were over, the two policemen concerned came to see me. They apologised for their conduct. They clearly saw that they had been wrong.

However, it was rather too late for them. Because of their conduct on a previous enquiry, both of them were demoted. One ended up as a policeman on the counter at the airport in Auckland. The other was placed in a very small country police station.

Now the trials were over, I felt that the matter was ended.

However, I was due for another surprise when I received a letter from the directors of the Housing Corporation asking for an explanation as to what had happened.

I then made a wrong decision.

One lesson I had learned from these experiences was never to be your own lawyer. I should have instructed a separate lawyer to respond, but instead of this I sent an eight-page letter setting out in full my side of the story.

For several months I heard nothing, though from time to time I rang the secretary of the Housing Corporation to find out its response.

Finally, about five months later, I rang to be told that a meeting of directors had decided to instruct all branches of the corporation to be careful in their dealings with us. I immediately told the corporation that if this letter went out, I would sue it for at least $20 million. The letter never left head office.

I heard nothing further from the corporation after that threat. It did modify its letters of instruction to its branches afterwards, but without referring to our company.

Again I thought that was the end of the matter, but I was due for another shock when Paul telephoned me to say that the Law Society auditor was inspecting the books of our law firm.

We had not had such an audit for 20 years, and on that occasion had been informed that our books were among the best in the profession. We had always prided ourselves in keeping our accounting books correctly. This is very important in a legal office because lawyers are investing millions of dollars on behalf of other clients and it is important that proper checks are carried out to ensure there is no fraud involved.

Each legal firm has an auditor, appointed by the Law Society, who checks the books regularly and it is only rarely that the Law Society auditor himself intervenes.

The man spent the best part of a month in our offices, inspecting the records, and said he was not entirely happy about our computer system. He did not seem to understand computerised bookkeeping.

About a month later I was horrified to receive a letter from the chairman of the disciplinary committee of the Law Society, telling me that the auditor had found irregularities in our books and I was given a week to explain them. Otherwise our firm could be prosecuted!

I rushed to see the chairman and asked him about the problem.

He said the auditor had noted that there were debit balances daily in our computerised accounts and that this was out of order.

The true situation was that each day our staff would print up the transactions which had occurred and these were sent to a centralised computer system controlled by the banks. The next day we would receive a print out. Invariably the first print out contained mistakes made by the operators employed by the bank and working overnight. As soon as the computer sheet was received by our office, our staff would check it for errors and make the corrections so that the following day they would disappear. On the next day we would go through the same procedure again.

I told the chairman that these were not debit balances, but simply input errors. I pointed out that they were corrected on a daily basis.

It was his turn to be surprised.

"We installed our own computerised system six months ago and instead of being a day late in our corrections, we are a month," he said. "Do you mean you are only a day late?"

I realised then that the auditor had not understood our system at all.

The chairman told me to forget about the whole problem and that he would take the necessary action. Not long afterwards, that particular Law Society auditor retired.

Yet again I thought that would be the end of the matter.

However, there was another surprise. I now received a letter from the Inland Revenue Department saying the company owed millions of dollars in arrears of tax.

The company had always been very meticulous in its tax returns. There were 12 companies in the group and each year some would report a profit and others a loss. After the losses were offset against the profits, tax was paid on the net amount. This was in accordance with New Zealand law.

Now the department was saying we had no right to join the companies together because they were different entities and under different control, even though they appeared to have the same shareholders.

When they brought the letter from the department to my office, my auditors were white-faced. They said this could be the ruin of the company.

I went to another room and prayed about the situation and the Lord gave me clarity of understanding.

One of the reasons I believe the Lord was able to bless in this regard was that, as a company, we had always tried to be honest in filing our tax returns. Each year, after our auditors had completed their audit, I would go through the accounts with them and ask about any matters which might be questioned by the Inland Revenue Department. I would then instruct them not to claim these items. I could always sleep well knowing that in years to come I would not face a major problem.

Knowing all of this, I felt prompted by the Holy Spirit to look up the original rules under which our companies had been registered. I found that when these rules had been prepared 25 years earlier, long before I had committed my life to Jesus Christ, His hand had obviously been on me. In each company I controlled the 10 voting shares, so I was in control of all companies.

As I looked at the law on taxation, I found that when a group of companies was controlled by one person, even though the share holding might appear different, those companies must be grouped together for tax purposes.

I called in both the auditors and my executive staff and told them the problem was now over.

Then I dictated the following letter to the Tax Commissioner:

"We have received your letter requiring us to amend our tax returns.

We are pleased, however, to tell you that your previous assessments have been correct at all times. This is because, according to the rules of our companies (copy attached), all the voting shares are controlled by the one person and, therefore, in accordance with the relevant section of statute, the companies must be combined."

I heard nothing further from the Tax Commissioner, but about eight months later our assessments were issued in accordance with the returns. So another crisis disappeared.

It took 18 months from the time the problem of the fraudulent wage certificates appeared for the situation to be resolved. It was a time of great trial.

It was only then that I was able to get on with publishing "Demons Defeated". Satan had done his utmost to prevent the publication of that book.

Now it is in 18 languages, with many more being added each year. No wonder Satan didn't want it published.

About six months after the problem had first emerged, I resumed public ministry. By then I had settled down and knew the Lord had been victorious in all of these trials.

Partly because of these sorts of hassles, and partly because of my yearning to serve God better, I was increasingly looking forward to the day when I could be free from my business and legal ties so I could devote myself full-time to the Lord's work.

Despite my activities, both in business and law, I was conducting upwards of 100 evangelistic meetings each year and had been privileged to see many thousands of people saved and healed and set free. Between 1980 and 1988 I was invited to be a speaker at seven world conventions of the Full Gospel Business Men's Fellowship and was privileged to be on the platform with many well-known leaders in charismatic renewal.

However, I had been practising law for 37 years and in the house building and land developing business for 26 years, and desired to be freed from them.

Wherever I travelled I had to keep in touch with my business every day. There were always decisions to be made. Sometimes I would be in the middle of a crusade when a major crisis would occur at home, making the two incompatible. Over the years, I continued to pray that God would set me free.

In 1971 a friend of mine, who had owned a major home building company, had sold out to a large New Zealand corporation.

At the time, I thought he was foolish, although he had received a considerable sum of money. However, four years later, when recession again hit the building industry, I realised how wise he had been.

In the mid 1980s, I realised that the day for me to sell out was near. I was initially approached by one of New Zealand's largest companies, but didn't quite feel ready.

A year later, I felt the time had arrived. New Zealand was experiencing a boom and the building industry was buoyant. I therefore instructed my executives to prepare a portfolio for a prospective purchaser and went back to the company which had approached me the previous year.

At the same time I was approached by another major organisation which wanted to buy the company, so I simultaneously placed the portfolios with both of them.

A couple of months later, the second organisation rang to say it wanted an appointment. It was interested in discussing a possible purchase.

I well remember the day I attended the meeting at that corporation. It had sprung up in the boom and had built billions of dollars worth of property around New Zealand.

As I sat in its beautiful main office, the directors gathered with me, the company's financial director began to read a report. It seemed to go on and on, containing a lot of figures, and I could not understand many of the points he was making.

After reading for some time, he suddenly stopped and said, "That is the best figure we can offer you."

I could not believe my ears. It was well in excess of our bottom figure and close to our asking price. As he named that figure, I felt a tremendous anointing fall on me. It was obvious the Lord was in this.

I tried to keep a straight face and turned to Paul and said seriously, "We will have to consider this offer."

The gentlemen present were very courteous and we left the room having bid them goodbye. As we approached the elevator, I turned to the director who was conducting the negotiations and said to him, "I need to tell you now that I have also offered this portfolio to another company."

With that, he said hurriedly, "Please come back into the offices again. We need to discuss this further." The company promptly raised its price.

Paul and I left the place bewildered. I could not believe that after all of these years I might become free of business.

The negotiations continued for some time. I approached the other company which had indicated interest. However, as it did not want to buy all our land and its offer was conditional, it was unsatisfactory.

Following further lengthy negotiations, I arrived at a suitable price with the first purchaser.

Then came the question of payment. The company wanted to delay the settlement, but I told the directors that their company could disappear just as fast as it had appeared. They were insulted, saying it was probably the strongest company in New Zealand and it would never disappear.

Having remembered my experience in dealing with the police over the fraud case, I told Paul that we must hire the best lawyer we could get to conduct the final negotiations.

As a result of the negotiations, settlement was reached and the price was paid.

Two years later, the great stock crash occurred in New Zealand. Ninety per cent was wiped off the value of every share in the stock market. Soon afterwards, the corporation which had purchased my company went into receivership. So much for companies which believe they will last forever.

Despite the crash, my former company survived and was sold to other purchasers who have carried it on.

When I sold out, I retired from legal practice. Having been released from both of these involvements, Pat and I have been free to travel throughout New Zealand and to many other countries, ministering the Gospel, and have rejoiced to see many souls saved. God is good.

FIFTEEN

Up and Down the Land

After selling my companies, I determined to preach the Gospel throughout New Zealand. To get this under way, I invited every pastor, minister and priest in the country to morning tea in their locality. About 5000 invitations were issued over a period of months and 1500 people attended.

I explained what I believed the Lord wanted me to do and received wide support from across the Body of Christ.

I believe any person who confesses with their mouth and believes in their heart that Jesus Christ is risen from the dead and seeks to follow Him is a member of the Body of Christ, whether they are Catholic, Methodist, Anglican, Pentecostal or from any other Christian denomination.

The Lord has mightily blessed the evangelistic meetings which have resulted. At times we have had up to 60 churches supporting them. I have been privileged to preach in every town and city in our country, as well as almost every hamlet. I have preached as many as eight times in some places.

I believe the function of the Body of Christ is to minister mightily to the unsaved. There are many out there who want to hear the Gospel of Jesus Christ and we should all individually respond to the calling of evangelism as the Lord directs us.

Sometimes, as a result of the evangelistic meetings, churches come together in fellowship for the first time. Committees arranging crusades often indicate that they are almost sorry when I arrive because they have been having such a wonderful time of fellowship with other churches.

When the Body of Christ moves together in this way, there is a great anointing and far better results are achieved.

Recently the Catholic Church in Wellington asked me to conduct a crusade. I was thrilled to be there. The Catholics worked in conjunction with the other churches in the locality and there was great blessing. Many unsaved came to the Lord.

A few months later, one of the principal Assemblies of God churches in Auckland asked me to conduct a crusade. Again, I said it must co-operate with other churches, which it willingly did. Crowded meetings were the result and many souls were saved.

My itinerant ministry through New Zealand has taken me to some unusual and interesting settings.

One such occasion was when one of the major Assemblies of God churches in Auckland asked me to conduct four crusade meetings and I found that the venue was to be my old grammar school.

It had been nearly 45 years since I had left the school, shaken the dust from my feet, and determined never to return.

I entered the hall that night with mixed feelings. I looked around the walls, and on the honours board I could see the names of many friends from my school days. Some had now died.

I went to a classroom to meet with counsellors and pray

with them, and nostalgia overwhelmed me.

As the meeting commenced, a great anointing fell and the Holy Spirit gave me an excellent message to preach. Many responded to the call to give their lives to Jesus, and major healings took place during the meeting.

As I left that night, I realised that only God could have brought me back there. God, who has a sense of humour, brought me back to the place I never wanted to visit, and there enabled me to proclaim His Word with power and see many lives touched.

Another time, I felt it was important to hold an outreach in a particular locality near Wellington. It was a very poor area and I felt a real pull from the Holy Spirit to go there.

I called a meeting of local pastors and asked for their support. However, when the time came for the meeting, my plane was fog-bound and I could not attend.

Later I learned that a number of pastors at the meeting felt it was not right for me to conduct crusades in that locality.

Towards the end of the meeting, a man stood up and gave a powerful prophecy to the effect that, "This is a move of God. Do not hinder it or prevent it. I have called My servant to this place." That ended the discussion.

When I subsequently met the committee, some members were still not convinced about the need for the meeting. I pointed out that there were 20,000 people living in the area and that they had a combined church attendance of only 500. I told them it was arrogant for them to believe they were ministering to a whole population, particularly as some of their churches were, in fact, about 50 kilometres from this local area. Apparently they had decided to take oversight over it even though they did not live there themselves!

On the afternoon before the first crusade meeting, I waited on the Lord and He gave me the names of 12 people who would be present at the meeting, and physical conditions which they were carrying.

At the beginning of the meeting I called for each of these people to come forward one by one. Most were Maori or part Maori.

The words of knowledge were devastatingly accurate and the power of God fell as I prayed for each person. A solemn hush fell over the meeting and there was a mighty presence of God.

When I had finished praying, the Lord said to me, "Don't preach. Simply make a call for those who want to give their lives to Me."

I made such a call and immediately there was a rush to the front. Those who had responded were taken outside for counselling and many of the counsellors, as well as those being counselled, fell under the power of the Holy Spirit.

I went on to preach and made a further call, and there was another wonderful response.

Since then I have had a number of return crusades in the same area. The meetings are always packed and many come to the Lord.

During one crusade, the local Catholic church invited me to conduct an outreach from its premises. The priest showed me the counselling room and it was clear it would be far too small so he immediately hired a hall across the road.

That night nearly 1000 people packed the church and over 100 who were totally unsaved came to the Lord.

Yes, the Lord does want us to listen to His voice and to respond boldly to Him!

Another area of particularly fruitful outreach and ministry in New Zealand has been the Youth for Christ Summer Harvest camps.

It all began one summer as I relaxed with my family on my yacht in the beautiful Bay of Islands, about 300 kilometres north of Auckland.

One hot day another vessel drew alongside and I recognised Ian Grant, the president of YFC New Zealand, on its deck.

He came aboard and shared with us a vision the Lord had given him concerning setting up a summer youth camp on a farm near the water in the Bay of Islands.

The Lord had earlier been speaking to me about the use of my own 1150 hectare sheep and cattle station, an extremely beautiful property with 7 kilometres of coastline, lovely beaches and high hills. Like all my assets, the Lord had long since shown me that it should be used as much as possible for His purposes.

It was clear the Lord had brought us together.

The following summer 1000 young people invaded our property for a week. The shearing shed was transformed into a kitchen with large ovens, while the overhead covered yards were transformed into a meeting place. Hundreds of bales of hay provided ideal seating.

The shearers' quarters became the headquarters of the whole operation, while buses transported young people from Auckland and were used to carry people across our property to the various beaches.

In the mornings there was a teaching session of an hour and then everyone was free to enjoy themselves until the late afternoon. In the evenings there was a further teaching session, with excellent music from the YFC band.

The young people, ranging in age from 14 to 30, were organised in groups of 30 with camp parents in charge of each group. They had brought their own tents and camped in open fields adjacent to the headquarters.

When Ian asked me to speak on the Sunday night, I decided to give my testimony. Although there was a considerable age difference, the young people listened intently as I shared about my life before I was born again and how God had brought me to a saving knowledge of Jesus Christ in 1971. As part of my story, I brought Pat to the platform and introduced her, along with other members of the family. The young people were very enthusiastic.

I then began to share that our body is to be the temple of the Holy Spirit and that God requires us to keep it pure and abstain from sexual immorality. After this I had an altar call.

A large number of people stood up and began to come forward, crowding the aisles. Following my usual practice, I asked them to get on their knees and repent before God. This they did willingly, and tears of repentance began to flow.

As this happened I realised something supernatural was occurring. I had experienced the wind of the Holy Spirit before in many meetings and I heard the voice of the Lord clearly saying, "The wind of My Spirit is coming from behind you now."

Suddenly there was a mighty outburst of noise. The wind of the Holy Spirit came across the platform and into the crowd and a titanic struggle erupted with the forces of darkness.

Hundreds of young people began to manifest demons. The noise was horrific. Some climbed up into the roof, wriggling like snakes. One climbed up the water tank.

As I looked around, I saw many people thrown straight off their hay bales on to the ground.

Then I looked over to Ian and saw him watching as the person on his left was suddenly swept backwards to the ground just as the person on his right fell forward. People all over the place were falling under the power of God while others were manifesting demon powers. Twenty young people rushed out of the building in fright and it took nearly an hour to locate them later.

Fortunately, some people in the crowd had experience in deliverance and they began to bind the spirit powers with me.

Ian was horrified at the scene. It was the last thing he had wanted or expected. Many of the young people present were from traditional church homes which were either non-charismatic or even anti-charismatic. Now their worst fears would be confirmed. One could envisage the reports that would go into those homes; never again would the young people be able to attend a YFC camp.

However, during that time many remarkable things happened. People subsequently testified of miraculous physical healings and many lives were instantly changed.

After order was restored, I resumed the altar call. The young people came forward again and I led them in a prayer of repentance and salvation. Then the power of the Holy Spirit came again and many were baptised in the Holy Spirit and spoke in tongues.

The camp parents were wonderful. They explained to many young people what had happened and restored their confidence. For others, however, it was clear what had happened — namely that there had been a major confrontation between the Holy Spirit and the forces of evil. The Holy Spirit had swept these away and, in the course of doing so, many had been set free, healed and delivered.

Two nights later it was testimony time.

I will never forget the young Maori girl who stood up and said that she came from a family of nine children, all of whom had served time in prison. Her father was a Mormon and her mother a Catholic. She could remember times when she had passed her mother's bedroom and seen her on her knees.

On the Sunday night her life had been instantly changed as she suddenly realised the reality of Jesus Christ and was born again. Now she was able to go home and tell her mother that she really loved her. There was not a dry eye in the building.

A young Maori man testified that he had come to the camp for a bit of fun. When he began to hear the girls shriek he thought this was rather "cool". However, he suddenly realised that something was writhing in him, beginning at his feet and going to the top of his head. He was the one who ended up on the top of the water tank.

He didn't know how he had got there, but this thing which had been in him had left him and now he had been converted to Jesus Christ and was determined to follow Him as Lord and Saviour. He knew the love, compassion and the power of Jesus Christ in his life.

I do not think anybody present at that meeting will ever forget it.

One young lady who was present did call a radio station noted for its anti-Christian stand and gave her account of the events. The station recorded her comments and asked if I would come and be interviewed. I suggested Ian came too.

When the record of what the lady said was played back on the station, instead of being something the enemy could use, it proved to be a real blessing. She said she had felt the forces of light and darkness meeting and she described the events. She told how one of her best friends had been instantly healed. Many calls flooded into the station and it proved a great witness for Jesus Christ. They were still talking about it on the station a week later.

The Summer Harvest camps on our farm continue annually. Nearly 10,000 young people have passed through and many thousands have been saved. All over New Zealand, young people come to me at my meetings and say how they were saved or blessed at the camp. Some have already become pastors.

God has been wonderful with the weather also. Each year we have been able to carry on, even though many parts of New Zealand have suffered bad weather.

Recently a priest from the Catholic Church approached us and said the church would like to have an observer present at the camp. We agreed and every year a priest attends and ministers to the young Catholics present.

Unquestionably, God has used this property. If we are willing to make ourselves and our belongings available, then God will use them.

As I look back on that first camp, I realise that Satan tried to destroy it from the outset. He wanted to discredit it because he knew the impact it would have on subsequent generations of New Zealanders.

It is to the glory of God that he failed.

I have also been involved, somewhat unwillingly, in a couple of "camps" which didn't bring such glory to God.

One was a four-day secular musical festival, called

Nambassa, where I was invited to take part in a Christian outreach at the festival. Not knowing what was ahead of me, I agreed.

As I drove to the festival site, I noticed road signs directing cars into various fields for parking. I travelled as close as possible to where the festival was being held, parked my car and stepped out to walk to the festival.

I walked through several fields and climbed over a number of fences, and as I did so the noise of the bands got louder and louder, the music echoing around the hills.

Finally I clambered up a hillside, and as I arrived at the top I looked down the other side and saw, to my amazement, three naked women rolling in the clay. They took no notice of me. A short distance further on, I found other groups of people frolicking naked. I was dressed in a suit — the contrast couldn't have been more marked.

As I came through a grove of trees, I saw a large number of tents, some of them very large marquees. Finally I found my way to the Christian tent, which was surrounded by marquees representing 35 Eastern religions. There were only two Christian marquees in the whole area.

A meeting was in progress in the Christian tent and people were sitting on bales of hay as the speaker preached.

All the onlookers were semi-naked or stark naked.

When the meeting finished, the Christians opened food queues and many hundreds lined up. About one person in three was stark naked.

That night, when I preached in the tent, it was clear that most of the 20,000 people present would not respond directly to preaching but had to observe signs and wonders. The Lord gave me some excellent words of knowledge and healings took place. People began to come forward in quite large numbers for salvation. Many of them wore no clothes at all.

There was a wonderful team of Christian young people involved in the outreach. They went around the camp and witnessed fearlessly about Jesus, often to people who were completely naked. Many of them responded to the Gospel.

The place was full of drugs. Marijuana could be smelt everywhere.

One morning, a police car came in to the grounds and as it stopped, I noticed two well-proportioned young ladies lean through the windows and leer at the policemen. The women had no clothes on and the policemen fled.

The Eastern religions were doing a great trade as people went in for hypnosis, spiritual rebirthing and all other alternative lifestyle forms.

However, the Christian message and the love of Jesus Christ entered the hearts of many.

After the third day we decided to have a water baptism. There was a beautiful river running through the camp and all those who were to be baptised gathered on the bank. Thousands of people watched as many of their young friends went under the waters of baptism to the sound of Christian choruses. Many testified of their changed life. The effect on the crowd was dramatic and a lot of the unsaved people could be seen weeping as they watched their friends baptised.

I came away from the festival feeling it was well worthwhile to have attended, though I can't say I enjoyed the experience. It was an eye-opener to me how others really lived, but also how the power of the Gospel has never changed.

A year later the same person who invited me to Nambassa asked whether I would attend another rock festival to be held the next month. Pat answered the telephone on this occasion, and he suggested she came with me.

We asked our four children to go. Two of them were married so this made a party of eight in all.

This festival, called Sweetwaters, was a hard rock festival about 100 kilometres from Auckland.

At least 40,000 people were attending the festival, held on a farm, with the hot February sun beating down day after day.

Although it was adjacent to a river, the site was not particularly beautiful. We towed our caravan into the festival and drove towards a site which we believed would be most suitable. There were already many caravans there, but while ours was commercially built, all the others were homemade.

We had just stopped when we were told by a bearded inmate to get out or else. We wasted no time in leaving and found another spot on which to place our caravan.

From the outset it was obvious that the young people present were there for a drunken party laced with drugs. Beer was everywhere and drugs were easily available.

Again we found two large Christian marquees, while about 40 Eastern religions were represented.

As the time wore on, more people became intoxicated and under the influence of drugs. There was not so much nudity on this occasion.

We went to a Hare Krishna tent where we saw people raising their hands to Hare Krishna, while in one corner a boy and a girl about four years of age were trying to have sex together. It was obvious they had watched their parents.

The atmosphere was deteriorating very quickly. As the rock bands played each night it became dangerous to walk through the auditorium area. People urinated on others and some threw full beer cans at all and sundry. The place was heading towards a riot.

Each night and day we preached in our tent and many people stopped to listen. I rapidly learned again that people would not respond just to the preaching of the Gospel, but needed convincing through signs and wonders. Accordingly, unless one operated in the word of knowledge and healed the sick and cast out demons, nothing much happened.

When a well-known preacher came to join us, I warned him that he must work in the gifts of the Spirit or he would get no response. I heard him preach a most marvellous sermon, powerful in every way. When he came to make his call, not a single person out of the audience of about 700 responded. He came to the back of the tent and wept. I reminded him that unless he worked in the power of the Holy Spirit, with signs and wonders, no results would follow. These young people were Gospel-hardened. Clearly many of them had come from Christian homes but had turned their backs on the Lord.

One morning, my daughter, Maria, asked what I thought of the strange grunting sounds going on in a tent close by. On investigation, I found about 40 people lying on the ground in a marquee making grunting sounds. All of them were naked.

I asked this leader, a guru, what they were doing. He said, "These people are getting spiritual rebirth." This was the satanic copy of being born again. The people were inviting demons into them, whereas when we turn to Jesus

Christ, we invite the Holy Spirit to come and live within us.

Another time we went into an adjacent tent and found people bowing down to a statue of Buddha. I could not believe that adult New Zealanders would bow to this golden statue and worship it.

Then we heard some young Maori people making a noise on another part of the grounds. They were very roughly dressed, and we thought they were mocking the Gospel because they were mentioning the name of Jesus Christ. As we got closer, we realised they were, in fact, preaching the Gospel. They came from a very poor district and here they were, fearlessly preaching the Gospel of Jesus Christ and leading people to the Lord. Their witness greatly encouraged us.

As the festival progressed, people were feeling the effect of the sun, alcohol and drugs. The surrounds of the toilets were torn down and people were defecating in the open area. A plea was made over the public address system to stop people under the influence of drugs diving head first into the toilets and drowning in the excreta. People were having to pull them out by their feet.

This is the degradation which Satan brings as people turn away from the Lord.

On Sunday we decided to hold an early-morning service in one of the natural amphitheatres. The stage was already erected and we had the sound system available to us. Hundreds of people were lying on the ground in a drunken stupor or waking up from the effect of the previous night's orgies.

A clergyman was in charge of the service. He spoke quietly and nobody appeared disturbed. Then my evangelist friend, Barry Smith, came to the platform. Without any ado, he quoted from 1 Corinthians 6:9-10: "Do you not know that the unrighteous will not inherit the kingdom of God? Do not be deceived. Neither fornicators, nor idolaters, nor adulterers, nor homosexuals, nor sodomites, nor thieves, nor covetous, nor drunkards, nor revilers, nor extortioners will inherit the kingdom of God."

The effect was electrifying. He had barely finished quoting this Scripture when those who had been lying comatose suddenly sat up and began to scream and shout. It was obvious the demons in them did not like this Scripture. Then they became threatening and started to come menacingly towards the platform.

Barry finished his sermon and it was my turn. I took over the microphone and spoke very loudly so these people could not shout me down. We claimed the protection of the blood of Jesus and proclaimed the Gospel loudly and clearly. Not surprisingly, a number of them came to know the Lord.

That night was to be the climax of the festival with the appearance of an Australian rock band, specialising in violence.

About 7pm one of the 38 policemen on the ground came to our tent. He was a Christian. "Please pray," he said. "There is a great danger of a riot taking place when this Australian rock band comes to play, and if it does so people will be killed."

Six of our young people went to the back of the main tent and began to pray. At 7.45pm they came out and told us that 15 minutes earlier two of them had had a vision of horsemen in the sky coming down over the main stadium. They were sure God had responded.

The "New Zealand Herald" music critic later wrote that everything had been ready for a great climax for the festival on the Sunday night, but at 7.30, when the Australian band appeared, suddenly the whole place went quiet and their playing was the most depressed he had ever heard. Nothing happened.

This was clear proof that God had acted and that the vision of the horsemen had been from the Lord.

On the Sunday night, it was my turn to speak.

The previous night, as I preached and prayed for the sick, at least 1000 non-Christians were gathered outside the tent. The sides of the tent were open so the whole crowd, both inside and out, was one group. About 500 Christians were sitting in the tent.

I proclaimed the Gospel, and then by the word of knowledge called several Christians and prayed for them. There was obvious healing and they were taken to the ground by the power of the Holy Spirit.

I had instructed the organisers to place a sign over my head proclaiming "Jesus is Lord." As the non-Christians watched me speak they had to watch this sign. I knew it would provoke the demons in them.

Then I told them that they were of the devil and their father was Satan himself. I told them this was so because they would go down to the Hare Krishna tent and raise their hands there, but when they heard the Gospel preached in our tent they would scream and yell. They began to get quite violent and noisy and my family began to get concerned for my safety.

At that point their leader, a very large man, appeared demented. As I prayed for the sick, he strode out of the crowd and stood in front of me. He was at least ten centimetres taller than I was and clearly under the influence of alcohol and drugs.

He looked at me and said, "Show me that power," referring to the power of the Holy Spirit which was causing people to fall.

I took a deep breath and said, "Lord, I have never done this before. Help me."

I raised my hand and placed it on this man's head and he fell on the ground under the power of the Spirit and did not move.

Behind him was one of his lieutenants. He was a smaller man, laughing and joking with the crowd and mocking me. However, when he saw his leader fall under the power of the Holy Spirit he wanted to run.

By now I was emboldened and told him to come back and laid hands on him. He, too, went down under the power of the Spirit.

Then another man came out of the crowd dragging his leg, which was in plaster. He said he had broken his leg three weeks earlier and asked if I could help him.

Having checked out thoroughly that his leg was, in fact, broken, I prayed for him. He fell under the power of the Spirit.

A few minutes later he got up and began to run. He was totally healed.

After that the meeting was really on. People from the crowd began to come forward in groups in order to give their lives to Jesus Christ. We were kept busy until 4 o'clock the next morning.

To my surprise, I found that many of the crowd who had been jeering and shouting at me had been brought up as Christians but had gone away from the faith. However, God had now convicted them of their sin.

The following year we attended the same festival again.

Here, again, God moved sovereignly in power.

However, it was clear that these festivals should not continue and we began to pray them out of existence.

The next one collapsed in financial failure before it even began. Two years later somebody else attempted to resurrect the same festival but again it collapsed. None has been held since.

SIXTEEN

The Anglican Enigma

The Anglican Church, of which I have been a member for nearly 40 years, has always been ambivalent towards the ministry the Lord has given me.

This is understandable. It is difficult for a church which is heavily structured and has an ordained priesthood to accept the fact that God can raise up a lay person as an evangelist with a healing and deliverance ministry without that person being specifically ordained for that purpose.

However, God is not bound by church or denominational structures.

Because of the prominent positions I had held as a layman in the church over many years, people were prepared to tolerate me even though they did not quite understand what I was up to.

The Holy Spirit has never led me to leave the Anglican Church. I believe God has been moving mightily within that church and by remaining a member of it, God has blessed me.

On many occasions, when I have travelled to other countries, the fact that I have been an Anglican has opened doors which otherwise would have remained closed.

Many people regard Anglicanism as a middle-of-the-road type of theology, so they feel they can relate to an Anglican without getting too threatened.

For many years, I visited my bishop each year to tell him of my activities and ask him to pray for me. One of these bishops has now retired, but in the early days of my ministry he said to me, "Bill, never let them give you a licence to preach."

I did not quite understand what he meant at the time, but have since realised that, had I been licensed, many within the church would have sought to interfere with the ministry.

I have always believed in being subject to leadership in the Body of Christ and have never wanted to do my own thing. Accordingly, wherever I minister, I submit myself to the leadership which has invited me. I have always been privileged to enjoy the support and prayers of my local church as well.

Some years ago, a major evangelistic conference was held within the Anglican Church. A number of bishops and other leaders from different countries were present.

When I was invited to speak, I said that rather than teach on evangelism I would prefer to carry out an evangelistic outreach one night. This request was granted and I was invited to speak in the cathedral.

That night the cathedral was packed and there was a real anointing in the meeting. The singing was excellent and there were several messages in tongues and interpretations. The Holy Spirit gave me clear words of knowledge and I prayed for the sick. Then I gave an evangelistic message and many responded to the altar call.

As I spoke, I wondered what some of the leaders were thinking, but did not worry too much about it.

Little did I know that they had decided to use the meeting to evaluate my ministry.

They gathered after the meeting and discussed what had taken place. I understand that various points of view were expressed, but the primary finding was that when the leaders looked around the meeting, they found that there were many ordinary and poor people present. Many had holes in their clothes. The liberal arm of the church usually claims these people as their constituency.

Finally, one leader spoke up and said he believed the meeting had been of the Lord.

Although I didn't receive any direct report of the evaluation, I was pleased to learn of its decision.

After being born again of the Holy Spirit I tried to testify to members of the Stewardship Council. I told them we were using the wrong methods for our fundraising, that the parishes should be renewed spiritually and then the money would flow in.

Some members listened but others could not understand. They had the same mind-set as I had before my experience with the Lord.

Then there was the matter of our vicar, an elderly man completing his final term of office. The only thing he knew about tongues was 1 Corinthians 14:19: "I would rather speak five words with my understanding, that I may teach others also, than ten thousand words in a tongue."

When we commenced our prayer meetings, we asked him to be present, because we wanted to retain our connection with the church and have its blessing and authority. He would usually attend the meetings for about half an hour, say a few words and then leave.

At that time we felt it was important to start an early

morning prayer meeting in our church, so each Thursday we went there at 6am. Several people would be present and the vicar would conduct communion at 6.30am.

This vicar retired and I asked the bishop if he would agree to the local vestry nominating the new vicar. He was happy about this, so I looked for a charismatic vicar who would be suitable for the church. I found such a person, brought him to Auckland and introduced him to the vestry, which offered him the position.

When I telephoned the bishop to say we had found a suitable man, I was astonished to learn that he had already appointed somebody to the parish. He assured me he would prove a very good person.

When this vicar, who was named Brian Jenkins, arrived we found he had come from a parish where there had been some evidence of charismatic renewal. He had regarded this with suspicion, but had not interfered with it.

He agreed to come to our prayer meetings each Thursday night and after a month his wife, Patricia, told us that she was ready to receive the baptism with the Holy Spirit though her husband was not yet.

We waited another month. One night our vicar went down on his knees and received the baptism with the Holy Spirit and spoke in tongues. His wife did likewise.

We continued the early morning prayer meetings throughout the following years and our vicar was a tremendous support.

At the end of three years, however, he felt he was being called to another parish. We were very surprised and disappointed by this.

He moved on to that parish and was there another five years before becoming director of the Church Army of New

Zealand, an evangelistic organisation.

When he joined our parish, he told us he was not an evangelist; that he was only called to take care of souls. However, during the period he was with us, God turned him around and he became one of the main evangelists for the Anglican Church of New Zealand. It is marvellous how God works in these matters.

Following his departure, a new vicar arrived. He was a traditional person and was Anglo-Catholic in his belief. He agreed to occasionally come to the meetings in our home. In the meantime we carried on the Thursday morning prayer meetings in the church and continued to pray for him regularly. He remained very cool towards renewal. After almost a year, as we were kneeling at the altar rail and praying, the Holy Spirit seemed to say to me that I should give $2000 to the church. After the service I went to the vicar and told him I believed the Lord was telling me to give that sum to the vestry. I thought he was going to weep. He told me the vestry was due to meet that night and it was exactly $2000 short and could not meet its accounts. He could see God was in it. He changed after that.

He had always said he did not want to see people fall over as they were prayed for, nor did he want anything to do with casting out demons. Shortly afterwards, however, while he was praying for somebody, the person fell under the power of the Holy Spirit. Not long afterwards, while he was praying for another person, a demon manifested.

He, too, was soon fully baptised in the Holy Spirit and became a powerful witness for the church.

At the end of three years he also decided he was called to a new ministry. He went to London and worked among the poor in the slums. God had done great things in our church and among our ministers.

The next vicar did not agree with our views at all. Although he carried on with the early morning prayer meetings, it was apparent that he was opposed to some of the things in which we were involved, in particular casting out demons.

After about a year, rather than cause further difficulty, I told him we would move to another parish and we have been involved in that parish ever since.

Between 1973 and 1976 nearly 100 clergy in the Anglican Diocese of Auckland were baptised in the Holy Spirit and spoke in tongues.

Unfortunately this charismatic renewal has not continued. I believe it is largely because the leadership of the church was not favourable. Although some parishes remain active in renewal, the majority are not. Unless the leadership of the church completely favours renewal in the Spirit, the Holy Spirit can be quenched.

Missing the boat spiritually, however, is not an area the Anglicans have exclusively to themselves.

Not long after being born again, I was introduced to the pastor of a very fast-growing Pentecostal church in Auckland and Pat and I grew to know and respect him and his wife.

One day he shared with me his vision to build a Bible college in Perth, Australia. He believed it should be in Perth because it is as close to Indonesia as it is to Sydney and he felt the Lord was saying he should train young men from Indonesia to be teachers of the Word.

After hearing of his plan, it seemed right to invite him and his wife to join us on a trip to Perth in order to find a suitable site.

Before we went, we called various church leaders together and at that meeting, my friend Doug Maskell, who had been helping me in the prayer meetings in my home, received a wonderful prophecy.

He was given a vision of Perth, with a wide river winding through it. Then he saw tree-covered hills, and a particular street, which was named, and finally a picture of a site with a blue caravan on it.

We all felt this was from the Lord.

In due course, Pat and I, together with our pastor friend and his wife, arrived in Perth.

Of course, the river Doug had seen in the vision was the Swan, a beautiful river flowing from the mountains and down through Perth itself to the ocean.

After a day or so, we began searching around the city to try and find the site Doug had received in his vision. We contacted a number of land agents but few of them seemed to know of a street with the name Doug had received.

As we explored one of the suburban areas of Perth, we travelled through the adjacent hills and were attracted to the office of a land agent on the main highway. We went in to discuss our problem with him.

He agreed to show us a number of properties but was also unsure of the name of the street.

As we travelled through various tree-lined roads, we came to a street which had a striking resemblance to the name Doug had been given.

We drove down the road and, as we came to an intersection at the end of it, a great anointing fell on us.

As we looked ahead, we saw a blue caravan on a property, just as Doug had described.

I paid a $50 holding deposit on the property and subsequently the church purchased that land.

However, for a variety of reasons the project never proceeded. In due course the church sold that property and the vision of the Bible college was never fulfilled.

Some years later, I was ministering in Indonesia and found there was an abundance of evangelists but very few teachers. The Holy Spirit said to me, "That is why I wanted a Bible college built in Perth to train teachers of the Word. This country desperately needs them."

It is sad to realise how we can sometimes miss God's purposes completely when we do not heed His voice.

SEVENTEEN

Miracle after Miracle

During more than 20 years of Christian life and ministry, I have seen God perform countless remarkable miracles of healing, deliverance, reconciliation and salvation.

God was, is and always will be a miracle worker, and as Christians we need to recognise that He is constantly wanting to see the miraculous — both in our own lives and, through us, in the lives of others.

In the West, we have often thought of the miraculous as being the domain of ministry in other, often Third World, countries. This is not my experience. Certainly the level of expectation and faith is higher at times in these countries, and so great signs and wonders do occur, but God no less wants to work miraculously in New Zealand or any other Western nation.

Nor is God restricted to the crusade or big meeting setting. He can work in any situation; all He requires is our faithfulness and we will see Him move.

A few years ago, I received a telephone call from a lady called Diane Parker, who asked me to pray for her son, Grant.

I arranged for Diane and her husband, Brian, to bring Grant to my office at my housing company. They carried him up the stairway and took him along the passage in his wheelchair.

A year earlier, Grant had become sick with a mysterious illness later diagnosed as ankylosing spondylitis. The doctors had done everything they could, but the pain-killing injections he was receiving were killing him. There appeared to be no hope.

Many people had suggested he come to me for prayer. However, the Parkers belonged to a church which taught that Jesus does not heal today, and viewed any prayers for healing with suspicion. They believed I might be a servant of Satan.

Finally, however, in desperation, Diane agreed to approach me and now they were in my office, hearts full of trepidation and not knowing what was going to happen.

As I talked with them, the Holy Spirit prompted me first to pray for Brian and Diane, and the next moment they were lying on the floor under the power of the Holy Spirit.

As they lay there, I began to pray with Grant and the Holy Spirit said, "Tell him to stand up," so I did.

From the floor Diane called out, "He cannot stand."

"Grant, please stand up," I ordered again. And he did.

Then I told him to begin walking. He took a few faltering steps, growing stronger with each one. His parents burst into tears.

Then he began to walk around the room, gaining confidence all the time, and the Lord said to me, "He will run."

So I opened the office door and said, "Go for a walk down the passageway, Grant." He walked the length of the passageway then back.

Then I said, "Run." He ran from one end to the other.

He was absolutely and completely healed. His parents

were in a state of shock, as were many of my staff who had seen Grant enter in a wheelchair only a few minutes before.

That afternoon the Parkers took Grant to their doctor, who was astounded and said it was a work of God.

That night they took him to their church. The people could not believe it. Grant ran up and down the stairs and all around the church. They felt him, touched him and in every way tested his healing.

The next day he was back at school. His teachers were concerned because they remembered how sick he had been and felt he would need special treatment. Instead of that he was able to immediately take up sport again.

When the Parkers took the wheelchair back to the hospital, the person in charge of the department concerned said, "Is the boy deceased?"

With joy his parents were able to say their son was totally healed.

The story in regard to the Parkers' church, however, was rather sad. Despite this healing the people still did not believe that Jesus heals today and the Parkers had to find a church where they could truly fellowship in the fullness of the Holy Spirit.

Three years later, Pat and I were on the ski slopes when we heard a shout from behind, "Is that you Mr Subritzky?"

I turned round to see Grant skiing merrily down the hillside.

Today he and his parents testify all over New Zealand and Australia as to the goodness of God. Many have turned to the Lord as a result.

Another remarkable healing miracle involved a critically ill Australian woman, Pat Shepherd.

I was speaking in Dubbo, New South Wales, with well-known English preacher, David Pawson. The crusade lasted five days and Pat Shepherd attended each nightly meeting. As she watched people getting healed, she desired healing for herself.

She had had a cortisone dependency for 21 years, brought on when she used the drug to deal with a condition known as lupus. God had healed the lupus following her conversion five years earlier, but she remained dependent on the cortisone. This led to her body becoming extremely fragile, and she suffered from diabetes and seven other major diseases.

When I called for people to come forward for prayer in the meetings, she could not do so because if she touched anybody she risked immediate bleeding.

Towards the end of the crusade, she began to reach out to the Lord.

I have found that if I give a general prayer for healing and ask people to place their hands on the part of the body affected, then God does great miracles, especially when there is faith. This faith usually arises as a result of signs and wonders earlier in the meeting and, of course, the preaching of the Word of God with belief.

This particular night, Pat Shepherd stood as I asked people to place hands on the affected part of the body and believe. As I prayed, she felt the power of God fall on her and she knew she was healed.

She had been taking considerable medication and now she felt she no longer needed it (I normally would not advise people to give up their medication without going to the doctor).

She stopped taking cortisone immediately, believing she was healed, and from then on her body totally recovered.

Six months later, having taken no medication, she went to a doctor. He did a thorough check and found that the diabetes had totally disappeared, along with all the other conditions.

Some years later, we videoed both Grant Parker's and Pat Shepherd's testimonies and wrote books on them as they confirmed the long-standing nature of their healing.

Yet another powerful miracle of healing came one day as I was ministering in a Women's Aglow group in Hastings, New Zealand. As I spoke, the Holy Spirit indicated that there was a lady present whose womb had reverted.

I asked her to come forward, and she had barely reached the front when she fell on the ground under the power of the Holy Spirit as God did a mighty operation on her body. Her stomach heaved up and down and it was clear something wonderful was happening.

Four years later, I was ministering in a meeting in Wellington and talking about how God could remove barrenness from wombs.

Suddenly this lady stood up and said, "It happened to me," and she came forward and gave her testimony.

She said that for four years she had tried unsuccessfully to conceive. Then I had prayed for her and she had had two sets of twins and one other child.

She assured me she did not want any more prayer for children, but she was grateful to God for His wonderful blessings in her life.

God's miracles are not restricted to healing, however.

He can move in any situation we choose to let Him.

One such experience I had involved a serious ecological threat to the waters near our Stanmore Bay beach house.

I learned of the threat as I returned from a day's fishing and was greeted by my neighbour, Ron. "Bill, do you realise they are going to tip sewage into this bay about 10 metres below low water mark?" he asked.

A hotel was being built on an adjacent hill, and as there was no sewerage reticulation available, the authorities had decided to allow sewage from the hotel to be dumped in the pristine waters of Stanmore Bay.

I was indignant, and contacted the local council member, who was quite rude.

So I called a meeting of local residents on the beach in front of our house and we decided to start a petition against the scheme.

I then telephoned the New Zealand Herald, the principal newspaper in our country, and the story became front page news. Each day for the next few weeks I gave the paper a fresh angle on the story. Later, the reporters said that they had never seen a story run for so long on a daily basis. Television and radio also carried the reports.

Within a week or 10 days 10,000 people had signed the petition opposing the dumping of the sewage.

We suggested that sewage for the whole peninsula be treated and put into the ocean some kilometres away from any populated area. In that way nobody would be affected and it would not ruin the environment.

The council, which said it would cost $15 million to build such a scheme, remained adamant that the scheme would continue.

I continued to pray about this situation and many others did likewise.

About a month after the start of the petition, the chairman of the council asked for a meeting. I consulted my friends, and many were very suspicious. They suggested I took a tape recorder.

When we sat down together, the chairman said he was a Christian. During the war, he had been imprisoned by the Japanese in the notorious Changi prison. While there, he had been born again and decided to spend the rest of his days working in public office.

He said he now agreed with our point of view and would request the council to drop its plans and build the treatment plant requested by the petitioners. I was astounded by this total turnaround. Until then, it seemed there was no common ground between us. Now, through prayer, God had changed the situation entirely.

If the initial scheme had proceeded, it would have cost millions of dollars to reverse it. Instead, Whangaparaoa peninsula has a sewerage scheme which doesn't affect its bays and which retains the beautiful clear water for the enjoyment of tens of thousands of people.

Yes, I do believe Christians can be involved in the preservation of the environment so long as it does not become an obsession and while we seek the guidance of the Lord in all our actions.

Another miraculous answer to prayer I received involved the selling of my expensive yacht.

After selling my companies, Pat said to me, "Bill, you have worked hard over the years. Why don't you build yourself another ketch?"

Since 1975 we had owned a 23-metre ketch called The Dove and had had much pleasure from it. I did not need much persuasion to go ahead with Pat's suggestion.

I called in a well-known boat designer and over the next year Paul and I began to design a new yacht.

However, by the time we had put everything into it, instead of a 25-metre yacht, it had become a 29-metre yacht;

instead of 50-tonne displacement, it was now 100 tonnes.

A year later, when the vessel was half built, I became convicted about it. I felt it was an unnecessary luxury and that I would never use it properly because I would be too tied up in ministry.

I began to pray about it and the Lord showed me clearly that it should be completed to the highest possible specifications so it would find a ready buyer.

Paul and I visited the Mediterranean and the east coast of the United States and studied vessels for sale. The choice of interior design was crucial. Would it be traditional or modern? We decided to go halfway in each case.

We hired the best designers in New Zealand and the best craftsmen to complete the vessel — three years after the initial design.

The vessel was beautiful, with one of the best systems in the world and highly-computerised navigation and communication systems. It had two engines and was equipped with every conceivable item of luxury.

We prepared excellent brochures and sent them to leading yacht brokers in the United States and one of them called us to say he had a prospective purchaser.

In September 1990, Ed and his wife, June, from the United States, walked on to the vessel and immediately fell in love with it.

After they decided to buy it, I said, "Now, Ed, I want to tell you why I am selling it," and explained my involvement with World Vision, my belief in Jesus Christ and my calling as an evangelist.

We got along extremely well in the two months before delivery — too well, perhaps, because when the time came to deliver the yacht to them in Fiji (because of the

New Zealand tax laws), Ed and June insisted on going to Suva in the yacht as well.

The passage between New Zealand and Fiji, about 1900 kilometres, can be very stormy and the last thing I expected was for them to want to go on the trip in case it put them off buying.

I had to travel to Singapore and Indonesia in order to preach, and the vessel was due to sail on a Saturday for Fiji.

On the Tuesday I rang Paul and enquired about the weather pattern and he said it looked as though a depression was coming over and would strike at the weekend.

I told Paul he should sail on the Thursday and the waters were like a millpond all the way to Fiji.

On the Saturday the yacht was to have departed, 140 yachts left Auckland on a race to the Bay of Islands. Only a few of them arrived. Many were dismasted and many were nearly wrecked in the storm that came through on that day.

I am satisfied that if we truly obey the Lord, He always blesses and protects. He certainly looked after us in this instance.

Ed and June went on to cruise in the South Pacific in that vessel.

Six months later they were back in New Zealand. One rainy night I was preaching to about 800 people in an outreach meeting some miles from where the vessel was lying at a marina. I had not noticed any members of the audience in particular, but when I made the altar call, to my astonishment Ed and June came forward to make public commitments to Jesus Christ.

It is interesting that they had to come to New Zealand and buy a ship in order to enter the kingdom of God. God's ways are not our ways.

One of the most special and personal miracles I have experienced concerned my relationship with my father.

During the years since my father had seized our furniture and belongings and threatened the sale of the house, our relationship remained cool.

Two years later his second marriage failed, and a year after that, he married another lady, Molly, who was rather older than himself. This marriage lasted 25 years.

As the years went by I began to see more of my father — usually when he wanted money to pay for overseas trips.

In the early 1960s he was taken ill with cancer of the bowel. The doctor operated on him and rang to say that he would not live for more than six months. I arranged for my father and Molly to go to the United States to the same health farm to which I had sent my half brother, Jack. However, after a couple of weeks he returned home.

Despite the doctor's comment, my father lived another 24 years. The doctor who had performed the operation died about a year after he had made the statement concerning my father.

During the subsequent years my father called occasionally at home, but I was always wary of him because I felt that all he and Molly wanted from me was more money.

In 1977 he was admitted to hospital for an operation on his hips. That night the doctor rang to say he was going to die. His heart was failing, his lungs were failing, his kidneys were failing.

I thought, "Well, my father is now 77 and he has had a fairly long life." I was not unduly concerned until later that night when the Holy Spirit began to convict me of my attitude towards him. Although I had appeared friendly towards him, I had never shown him God's full love.

I began to pray that God would spare my father until

such time as I could show him the love that I should have done years before.

The next day, the doctor said my father would die that night. His heart, lungs and kidneys were failing.

But he clung on, and I continued to pray.

For weeks his mind was scrambled and he was semi-conscious. He neither recognised nor spoke to anybody.

After three weeks in intensive care with no improvement, the doctors put him in a small room at Middlemore Hospital in Auckland for eight weeks.

I visited him every day and each time the young doctor would step out of his little office opposite my father's room, and go with me to see him. He was never any different. His mind was scrambled and he was full of tubes. The doctor would always say, "He's going to die, you know."

Each day I continued to pray that the Lord would grant my father an extension of life so at least there could be a reconciliation.

At the end of eight weeks, as I walked along the long corridors of the hospital one day, the audible voice of the Lord spoke to me and said, "I have healed your father. I have given him another seven years of life."

I quickened my step and as I approached the office where the doctor usually sat he came out of his office, gave me a strange look and said, "Come and see your father."

We crossed over the corridor into the little room, but when I looked at the bed there was no sign of my father.

Instead, he was sitting down in a chair, and when he saw me he jumped to his feet, looking perfectly normal, stretched out his hand and said, "Hello Bill," as though nothing had happened.

I was astounded.

"What did you do with him?" I asked the doctor.

"We gave up on him," he said. "We thought he would die, so we took all the tubes out of his body. But instead of dying he was instantly healed."

My father was discharged from the hospital the next day.

But that was not the end of the story.

About the same time a new telephone directory had been issued and I discovered that a quirk in the computer system meant my address had been changed and I was incorrectly listed. It would be another 18 months before the new directory came out.

I knew many people would be trying to ring me and was quite angry about this situation. In ministry, one receives calls from all over the world from many needy cases.

My father and I shared the same initials and when he returned home from hospital his phone began to ring incessantly. People were looking up W. A. Subritzky in the telephone book and my father was the only one listed with these initials.

As soon as people heard his voice on the telephone, they poured out their problems. My father found himself counselling other people and, in fact, praying for them. Some calls came in the early hours of the morning. This went on until the new directory was printed. During this time my father was thoroughly saved.

I never told my father that the Lord had given him another seven years.

Every Friday when I was in Auckland, I would call on him and pray for him. At first his knees gave out, but then they were healed. Then he went deaf, and was healed.

Each Thursday night when we held a family gathering,

he and Molly had a meal with us all. Our fellowship grew and a real bond developed between us.

One day when I visited, Molly was in bed ill. I had tried to witness about Jesus Christ to her many times but she was not interested. On this particular day a righteous anger came over me. I saw that she had not long to live and that she was headed for eternal damnation.

I walked into the room and confronted her while she lay in bed.

"You know, Molly, you have never given your life to Jesus Christ and you are facing death," I said. "I want you to know you are heading straight for hell unless you repent."

She sat bolt upright, stunned by my comments.

My words had finally got through. At that moment she repented and gave her life to the Lord and shortly afterwards passed to be in His presence.

The Bible says in Jude 22-23: "And on some have compassion, making a distinction; but others save with fear, pulling them out of the fire, hating even the garment defiled by the flesh."

Sometimes we have to see people saved by fear.

After Molly's passing, my father lived alone in his home. I provided him with a full-time housekeeper who visited him daily during daylight hours and took care of his needs.

As the years went by, I periodically met his doctors, two of whom told me that my father would die shortly. I knew, however, that God had given him those seven years. Both of these doctors died before my father.

After seven years, my father went into hospital for a routine check up. He was feeling fine and I well remember that when I visited him on a sunny Monday afternoon, he was sitting on the side of his bed swinging his legs and looking very happy. I did not know the full reason for his happiness, but later learned that he had just proposed to the housekeeper. He was 84 years old so there could not have been very much wrong with him.

However, about 3 o'clock the next morning, the telephone rang at our home. It was the nurse in charge of the ward.

"Just now your father gave a little cry and he was gone," she said.

The seven years had elapsed. God had fulfilled His Word. My father and I had been reconciled and our family and our grandchildren had grown to know and love him.

God's healing of our relationship was just one of many miracles He has done in our family.

Some years ago, my daughters, Janne and Maria, thought of having a Subritzky family reunion.

Since the Subritzkys first settled in New Zealand in 1830, the family had grown to perhaps 1000 strong.

We sent invitations to as many as possible, inviting them to a function at our home. We erected a large marquee over the tennis court and about 500 came.

I found that many of my relatives were part Maori, as some of the early Subritzkys had married Maoris. It was great to see people from a variety of backgrounds all claiming the name of Subritzky.

However, I was unsure of some of them. When they arrived with leather jackets and powerful motorbikes, I wondered whether we should not, perhaps, have screwed down a few more things!

However, the weekend went very well and on the Sunday morning I was asked to conduct a church service.

I preached the Gospel and gave my testimony. Then I told those present that, although we had all descended from the same bloodline, there was a far better bloodline that we could be born into — namely the family of Jesus Christ. I then gave an invitation and over 70 responded.

I believe we should be fearless in our presentation of the Gospel of Jesus Christ at every opportunity.

A close friend of mine testified to a person aged 65 and he gave his life to the Lord.

"Why didn't you give your life to the Lord before?" my friend asked.

"Nobody ever told me," came the reply.

I wonder how many people have never been told by Christians around them of the love of Jesus Christ.

Before the reunion, it was decided that everybody would bring their family Bibles.

The most interesting one belonged to the family of my grandfather's brother, who had been a Brethren preacher. He had travelled throughout New Zealand in a horse and cart, preaching the Gospel, and at the back of the Bible he had noted all the places where he had proclaimed the Gospel.

Now, nearly a hundred years later, I had been doing the same thing.

I have no doubt that, just as curses can come down in the generations of those who hate the Lord, so indeed the blessings of God follow down the generations of those who love Him!

EIGHTEEN

Standing Against the Devil

Shortly after I was born again, I visited a local Pentecostal church and listened to an anointed preacher named Frank Houston. At that time he was superintendent of the Assemblies of God New Zealand.

I listened in awe as Frank detailed various miraculous healings and experiences in the course of his ministry.

He was obviously a man of wide experience in the Lord and I came away with a sense of awe about him. Little did I dream that one day God would call me to minister alongside him.

A number of years later, Frank felt called to go to Australia and establish a number of churches.

One day I received a call from the Full Gospel Business Men's Fellowship of Australia, asking me to speak in its next Australian conference at Brisbane. It was only when I received the brochure that I found my co-speaker was Frank Houston.

The first night I spoke about repentance and a number of people came forward, one of whom was the son of a prominent Christian.

The next night Frank ministered. When he had completed his message, we agreed to stand together at the front of the meeting and work in the word of knowledge.

The Lord was gracious. First He gave Frank a word, and a person was called out for prayer. Then He gave me a word, and we operated alternately in this manner for some time.

As the meeting was drawing to a close, a noise began on the left in the front of the meeting. I looked over and saw a man manifesting in demonic power.

As he did so, he was propelled into the air and began travelling towards the stage. He must have been about a metre off the ground and moved at least five metres. Frank shouted, "Get out of the way, Bill." The man landed where I had been standing.

I began to pray for him in order to cast out the demonic power. For nearly an hour this man slid under the chairs as the demon caused him to wriggle like a snake. At the end of that time he was set free.

The only objection to this event came from a woman who entered the meeting during the deliverance. She began accusing me and said, "Leave the poor man alone. Leave him alone." I later learned she was a witch.

The episode put the meeting into shock. Many believe Christians cannot have demons, and the man who had manifested had been brought up in a Christian church, was born again and had received the gift of tongues.

The next morning his father thanked me for the transformation that had taken place in his son and at breakfast that morning the man who had been delivered stood up and gave his testimony. It had a powerful impact on the whole gathering.

As a result of his testimony, many other Christians came forward for deliverance. The theme of the conference had been spiritual warfare and at the end of three days we had certainly seen plenty of it.

During the conference one man came to me and said he had once been a pastor but now, in his 60s, he had lost his ministry.

As I looked at him, the Holy Spirit said, "Ask him about his mother." As I did so, a voice spoke out of the man, "I hate her."

I asked him about the age of his mother.

"She is in her early 90s and she has always dominated me," he said.

I took him up into the hotel room and began to pray for him. The back of his neck quivered and he shook like a dog coming out of the water. I commanded the mother spirit to come off his neck and he repented of his attitude towards his mother and began to forgive her.

With that, he vomited across the carpet and a great demonic power left him. He stood up absolutely free.

At the end of the conference, Frank and I felt we had had enough of demons for a while.

Next we were scheduled to speak at another Full Gospel Business Men's conference in Geelong near Melbourne. As we travelled south, we received a message to the effect that the theme of that conference would be deliverance from oppression. We could not believe our ears.

For the first two days we ministered on many subjects, but it was apparent that sooner or later we had to face the issue of deliverance.

On the Saturday afternoon I taught in that area and Frank followed me. When he had finished, he asked those who thought they needed deliverance to come forward and about 80 responded.

Frank then said he had to catch a plane back to Sydney in time for his church service the next morning, and he would have to leave the situation in my hands.

As I prayed for these people, many fell on the ground, writhing like snakes. For two hours I prayed for as many as possible but I couldn't achieve everything on my own.

That is why I always require a large number of counsellors to help in my crusades. They must be trained in healing, deliverance and baptism with the Spirit, as well as encouraging people in salvation.

Fortunately, there was a person skilled in this area and many people were able to be delivered after the conference.

Today Frank Houston pastors a very large church in Sydney and his son also pastors another large church. God has rewarded Frank's faithfulness.

Every Christian needs to be taught about the reality of Satan and his demonic attacks. Without this understanding we run the risk of being oppressed and rendered ineffective in the ministry to which God has called us.

On one occasion during crusade meetings in New Plymouth, New Zealand, I was staying in a motel close to the centre of the city. I took little notice of the motifs symbolising Maori gods on the exterior of the room, although I had long since learned that when I stay in motels I should first cleanse the rooms thoroughly in the name of Jesus Christ. Various spiritual forces can lurk in those rooms because they are often used for immoral purposes.

On this occasion, however, I overlooked doing it.

One morning, after reading my Bible on the bed, I noticed blood stains where I was sitting.

I immediately began to think I had a problem in my bowel, remembering that at the same age my father had similar symptoms as a result of bowel cancer.

I prayed about it and also asked others for prayer. Then I went to the doctor for a check-up.

It took nearly two weeks to get the results of these x-rays, and even when they were clear it still did not mean I was free of any condition.

The doctor then suggested that I be examined by a specialist. Again I had to wait for about two weeks for this.

Throughout this time the devil had a hey-day. He attacked my mind in every possible way, and I had to take hold of the name of Jesus and not let go. I remembered that Jesus said the devil was the father of lies.

About six weeks after that morning in the motel, I was ready to see the specialist. There had been no further bleeding. The doctor was a kindly man, but as I looked at him I could see a spiritual power around him. He examined me at length and said, "I can find no trace of any problem there."

As he said these words, I saw a spiritual power manifest. As a person who operated constantly on people with cancer, a demonic spirit seemed to follow him. As he spoke to me, I could see his face change and it was almost as though the spirit was expressing disappointment.

Needless to say, I was relieved and grateful to the Lord for His protection. It was out of experiences like this that the Lord led me to write a book called, "How to Overcome Fear." I have long since learned to hold on to the Word of God when I am under attack and to believe every part of that Word.

One Scripture which always helps me in these circumstances is Psalm 118:17, "I shall not die, but live, and declare the works of the Lord."

Demonic attacks can come upon us from the most unlikely sources — including Christians.

Some years ago, when opening a letter from a person I

did not know, I felt an oppression come on me. The writer was questioning my stand on the issue of healing and was asking a number of specific questions. I carefully responded to each point he raised.

Then I received a further letter from the same man, raising further points, which I again responded to.

Then a third letter arrived questioning other points. Again I responded at great length.

I heard nothing further until about a year later when I found that a group of young evangelicals at Auckland University had produced a small book attacking my ministry. When I read the first two pages, I realised the person who had written to me had been acting on behalf of a committee, which had taken portions of my replies and put them together with writings from my book "Receiving the Gifts of the Holy Spirit". By doing so, they had constructed a totally false picture of my beliefs.

By the time I reached the fifth page I felt angry and sickened and resolved to read no more and put it to one side.

The book was fairly widely distributed among the Christian community.

I prayed for those who had written it and especially that God would bless them. In that way I obtained a complete release.

About seven years later I received a call from some young evangelicals asking me to minister on the campus of Auckland University. Immediately my mind went back to that book, but I agreed to go anyway.

When I arrived at the theatre, I found it was packed with people.

I stood on the platform and pronounced my belief in the risen Jesus Christ, in His atoning death and in God's love. Then I reached out for a word of knowledge.

The Lord indicated that in the back row there was a person suffering from asthma.

At that a young man rushed forward and stood defiantly in front of me.

"I am leader of the Atheist Society in this university," he said. "See what your God can do for me!"

I was taken aback and said, "Have you really got asthma or are you just trying to make a fool of me?"

He said I could ask anybody around him and they would confirm that he did.

I began to pray for him and as I laid hands on him I felt his whole body trembling. A spirit of fear within him began to manifest and I knew instantly that I had the authority needed, in the name of Jesus Christ, to deal with the situation. Then he felt the power of God coming through him and he went back to his seat very subdued.

The Lord was gracious enough to give me other excellent words of knowledge. I then gave my testimony and made an altar call and many came forward to receive salvation.

My hosts were delighted and I shared with them what their predecessors had written in the book.

They told me God had moved mightily in charismatic renewal among the young Christians in the university and no longer were these matters questioned.

I received a lovely letter of thanks from them, including an apology on behalf of their predecessors.

That attack on my theology, integrity and authenticity in ministry had been a low-point for me.

However, God had graciously turned the situation around to the point where I could minister at the university in the very areas for which I had been attacked.

However, while there are occasional critics of my type of ministry, there are far more people who are eager and hungry to learn how to minister in the Spirit.

Some years ago, I received a telephone call from Chris Mungeam of Sovereign World book publishers in England, who wanted to republish "Demons Defeated" in England.

In due course, this and other books were published by Sovereign World in England and widely distributed.

Later, Chris faxed me and suggested I went to England to speak on deliverance from demons, as by now some of my books had been widely read. In due course, Pat and I arrived for five major meetings around England.

Chris has remarkable communication skills. His wife, Jan, also has a wonderful outreach through Sovereign World Trust, an organisation which distributes Christian books free to needy nations.

The Lord woke me about 3 o'clock on the morning of the first scheduled meeting and spoke specifically that I was not to start with deliverance, but with salvation, then baptism with the Spirit, then gifts of the Spirit and finally deliverance.

About 1000 people came to each of the five meetings, many of them Christian leaders. I followed the programme I believed God had given me and there was great blessing.

I told Chris that if I ever returned to England I would need four days to give wider teaching. Not long afterwards, he contacted me to say he believed we should hire the Brighton Centre at Brighton for such meetings.

I didn't anticipate having such a large hall, but Chris pointed out that whereas the usual cost would be about $75,000, if we could satisfy the Brighton council that we were using it for a Christian outreach, the cost could be reduced to as low as $5000.

The first such conference was held in 1990 and nearly 3000 people attended from all over England and Europe. Peter Horrobin of Ellel Grange healing centre in England and New Zealanders Graham and Shirley Powell shared the platform with Pat and myself.

There was a great anointing on the conference and many lives were dramatically changed.

On the Wednesday night of healing, Peter spoke first and I followed. Then I asked the Holy Spirit for words of knowledge and the power of God began to fall across the meeting. The Lord directed me to a man in the third row who had a heart condition. I brought him on to the platform. When 3000 people are watching and expecting something to happen, we have to rely entirely on the Holy Spirit.

I sensed no anointing around this man and knew something was blocking it. The Holy Spirit then gave me a specific word that there was a spirit of death on him. I cast it from him and immediately the anointing began to fall.

Little did I know that three months earlier he had died in an ambulance on his way to hospital and had been resuscitated by medical staff.

Shortly after the man left the platform, it was clear that he had received a tremendous healing as he ran and danced around the place.

He came to the next conference in Brighton a year later and testified to a totally changed life and complete healing, both from the heart problem and asthma.

At the same conference, I received a word of knowledge that God was healing a man of a back problem. The Holy Spirit said the person, named John, was standing behind me in the meeting. I turned around to look for John but nobody responded to the call.

There was, in fact, a John with a back problem behind me, but he did not realise it was him. He was the cameraman, and he was moving his camera across the meeting looking for the person called John.

Suddenly he realised he was the person being called and he raised his hand. He had had a back problem for 20 years.

The Holy Spirit told me to get him to place his hands behind the back of his neck. He did so, and later testified that he could not remove his hands once he had placed them there. He then slid under the seat as he fell under the power of the Holy Spirit.

At a similar conference a year later, John testified of his complete healing.

At the next conference, we agreed to have another night teaching on healing. We followed the same procedure and I asked the Holy Spirit to give me further words of knowledge.

As I moved through the meeting, He directed me to three specific conditions, including a person whose arm was permanently bent.

I took these people on to the stage and prayed for them as the Holy Spirit directed. They all fell under the power of the Spirit and were there for some time.

Then a young man rushed to the front of the meeting and on to the platform. He said he had a back problem and had been prayed for by many people but could not be healed. He did not know even why he was up on the platform.

Usually I pray only for those in a public meeting to whom the Holy Spirit directs me, but he seemed insistent and I asked the Holy Spirit for direction. He said, "Do not pray for his back, but place your hands on his neck and command the demon of rejection to leave him."

I did so. There was a terrible scream for nearly a minute as that demon left him. Then the Holy Spirit directed me to lay my hands on his stomach. Again a powerful spirit manifested. Then the Holy Spirit said to take his right arm and command a spirit to leave from there. The same thing happened.

Finally I prayed for his back and he appeared to receive complete healing.

When I began to question him further, he was completely changed. It was as though some veil had been lifted from him. He looked around and suddenly realised he was standing in front of 3000 people. He hung his head and, after receiving some encouragement, was led off the stage.

I believe Satan drove this man on to the stage to challenge the ministry. It was obvious that people were being healed, but the devil wanted me to be diverted. If I had immediately prayed for this young man's healing he probably would not have been healed. But by listening to the Holy Spirit and commanding the demons to leave him, the plan of the devil was uncovered. Many saw complete and specific deliverance take place before their eyes as Satan's trick was unveiled.

The other three people, who were still on the floor, now stood up. All of them had been healed of their physical infirmities.

Little did we know that at that first Brighton conference there had been a man from Hungary whose father had prayed for 40 years that a healing centre would be established in Budapest.

Through a series of circumstances, he telephoned Peter Horrobin and invited him to Hungary, and from this visit arose a clear vision to have a conference in Hungary and invite pastors from as many Eastern European countries as possible.

This conference took place immediately after the second Brighton conference.

Eight hundred pastors and leaders from Latvia, Lithuania, Estonia, Russia, Ukraine, Poland, East Germany, Hungary, Bulgaria, Yugoslavia, Denmark, Finland and Romania attended.

One of the most interesting aspects was that the conference was held in the former Communist Party headquarters in Budapest. Two years earlier, the party had met there and, after 30 years of rule, decided to hand the government of the country over to others. The party changed its name and its membership fell from 700,000 to 40,000.

For 30 years, communist leaders from all over Eastern Europe had met there for conferences. May Day processions had been held outside the premises. A Hungarian pastor told us that as a lad he was required by law to march in these processions, even though he hated doing so. I have since learned that my son-in-law, Kalman, who was born in Hungary, had done likewise.

Now communism had ended, a great statue of Lenin which had stood in the area had been torn down and the building was being used for God's glory.

At that conference I learned more of the power of videos. I found people from Romania and other countries had been watching my teaching videos, even though they were in English, and had been greatly blessed by them. This encouraged me to begin dubbing my videos into other eastern European languages.

The conference facilities had multilingual channels for translations and were ideal for our purposes. We were able to put interpreters in booths and provide simultaneous translations for the various nationalities represented.

During the conference, it was clear that there was an intense dislike between the pastors from the various countries. The history of Hungary and its adjacent nations, including Russia, is one of bloodshed, repression and brutality.

However, as the power of God continued to fall in the conference, many pastors were convicted of their attitudes. Amid great weeping and repentance, real reconciliation took place. For this reason alone, the conference was justified.

Communism and other "isms" may come and go, but the kingdom of God lasts forever!

NINETEEN

The Work Goes On

It is now more than 20 years since Pat and I were born again.

During that time we have found that persistence and obedience to the Lord always brings results.

Many times we have gone to meetings feeling as though it was the last thing we wanted to do, but God has intervened and sovereignly blessed.

I thank God for the gifts of His Spirit, which I constantly try to exercise.

By using these gifts we follow the example of Jesus Christ.

For example, in John 4:17-18 Jesus startled the woman at the well when He told her she had had five husbands. The woman had not told Jesus anything about herself, but He knew her history.

As a result of Jesus giving this word of knowledge, the woman proclaimed Him as the mighty prophet of God.

Another time, Jesus was confronted by Pharisees who had with them a woman caught in adultery. He waited for a word of wisdom from God as to how He should deal with the situation. He always carried out what His Father told Him to do. This is how we should act and the Holy Spirit will, indeed, speak to us.

As we look at John 8:6-12, we find that on both occasions Jesus was challenged by the Pharisees about this woman, He stooped down and waited for the Father to give Him clear direction as to what He should say.

The first time, He rose and said, "He who is without sin among you, let him throw a stone at her first."

The second time, when He found everybody had left, He said to her, "Neither do I condemn you, go and sin no more."

In Acts 5:1-9, the Apostle Peter operated in the gift of discerning of spirits when he told Ananias that Satan had given him a lying spirit. Similarly, in Acts 16:16-18, we find that Paul discerned the spirit of divination on a certain slave girl and commanded it to leave her.

These and other gifts are vital in any ministry which is going to operate in the power of the Holy Spirit.

When leading an evangelistic meeting, I seek to listen carefully to what the Holy Spirit is saying. I believe He will always give clear direction as to how we should pray.

I often find that before the meeting He gives me names of people who will be present and their physical problems. Furthermore, He sometimes gives me the locality in which a person is living.

At the appropriate time in a meeting I call these people forward one by one and pray for them. It is always important to pray for the correct person.

Sometimes more than one person will respond to the same name and condition.

I then wait on the Lord and He gives me a further name which relates to one person only. In that way I find the person the Lord is seeking to touch at that moment.

I have had as many as three people respond to the

same call, and I have had to ask the Lord for several words of knowledge to find out exactly who He is speaking about.

Once, two men responded to the same word of knowledge and both moved forward in the meeting.

I asked the Lord for a further name and He said, "Ask for the person whose father's name is John." As I did so, one of the men responded, and at that moment he fell to the ground under the power of God. It was a powerful demonstration.

The Lord also gives specific words of knowledge about people, and even tells me the row in which they are sitting. For example, He will say that in the ninth row there is a person with a kidney condition, or in the 11th row there is a person who has recently had a heart attack. I go to these rows and call for the person to come forward. I have learned to persist with a word of knowledge, to encourage those who are reticent to respond to God's call.

As the meeting progresses, the power of the Holy Spirit begins to fall and He touches various people across the meeting.

One night I watched as a girl's eyes were straightened. Another night a woman began to scream because she had been blind for three years and had now been healed. On another occasion, in Melbourne, the Holy Spirit began to speak to me about a deaf person. Suddenly a woman screamed in a very loud voice and when we went to her we found that she had been deaf in one ear for 50 years and had now been healed.

I always believe for the anointing of the Holy Spirit to fall in a meeting. Sometimes there has to be powerful praise and worship before this happens. One must always ensure there is an anointed singing group present and the songs must be carefully chosen.

In every meeting I expect the fragrance of the Holy Spirit, as Jesus Himself moves through the meeting by the Holy Spirit.

I fervently believe in Psalm 45:8, "All Your garments are scented with myrrh and aloes and cassia, out of the ivory palaces, by which they have made You glad."

I also expect the wind of the Spirit to be felt by many people across meetings.

I do not go on what I feel. I believe if we act in faith, the feelings follow.

Recently I was telephoned by a weeping mother whose son had been involved in an accident three weeks earlier and was now being kept alive by a machine. That day the doctors were to decide whether to take him off it and let him die.

I rushed to the hospital and met the mother and the mother of the man's girlfriend. Both women were Christians and had been praying fervently.

The girlfriend was also there, looking very haggard. She had never committed her life to the lordship of Jesus Christ.

I went in with the two mothers and laid hands on the young man. He was lying motionless on the bed while the machine kept his heart going. It looked hopeless. However, I continued to pray in faith.

When I left the room, the Holy Spirit said, "Go back again and pray yourself." I went and again laid hands on the young man.

A few hours later I received a telephone call to say his eyes had flickered, so the doctors had decided not to turn off the machine. The next day his eyes moved.

I heard nothing more for two months.

Then, at the close of one of my evangelistic meetings, a radiant young lady came forward.

"Do you remember me?" she asked. "You prayed for my boyfriend in the hospital three months ago. He was the one on the machine."

I could not believe the change. Clearly she had given her life to the Lord and was now completely different.

I asked her how her boyfriend was keeping.

"Oh," she said, "he is just fine. He's home and did not come to the meeting tonight because he has a headache. Otherwise he is perfectly well."

Yes, God is the God of miracles today.

When I sold my companies, the Lord gave me clear direction to buy a complete video set-up so I could make my own videos. We built studios and employed staff. I began to take videos of our evangelistic outreaches and teaching meetings.

In the last three years we have sold over 10,000 videos. I give authority for them to be copied by other people because I do not believe the ministry belongs to me. They are widely used in Africa and many other countries.

At the same time, the Lord encouraged me to begin writing and now books like "Demons Defeated" are translated into many languages. Nearly every month I hear of people translating them into another language.

I believe that if we will take a small step for the Lord, He will take a large one for us. He requires us to do the small things faithfully and then He will do the rest.

As we preach the Word, we never know whose heart we are touching.

I thank God for a man like Harry Greenwood, whom God took as an unsaved sailor on a naval vessel and touched mightily.

Recently the president of the Auckland University Students' Association, an organisation of 18,000 students, came to one of our meetings. He had been elected on a programme of legalising drugs and allowing their free distribution in the university campus as well as many other so-called freedom programmes.

He had not intended to come that night, as he and his girlfriend were going to see a film. However, his mother, a Christian, encouraged him to go.

As he watched people being healed, the power of God began to fall on him. He came forward with his girlfriend and was powerfully converted.

He went back on to the university campus and, instead of trying to legalise marijuana, he opened prayer meetings. One can imagine the impact this has had on the campus. He also experienced widespread opposition, with articles attacking him regularly appearing in the student magazine.

Despite these attacks he was elected for a second time by a record majority. Only the Holy Spirit can convert a person in this way.

Recently that man shared a platform with me at an evangelistic outreach. He had been well and truly born again.

We have seen God demonstrate His power many times among young people.

On one occasion, in the Wellington Town Hall, a young man came up for prayer. He had been suffering from a stomach ailment for a number of years. As he stood before me, the Lord said the word "pot."

"Spirit of pot, leave this man," I commanded.

He fell down and slithered backwards across the floor for about 10 metres. Then he manifested violently. We prayed for him for some time and finally he was delivered of the spirit of pot, or marijuana.

Only God can do these things. As we are obedient to Him and submit to one another, God is able to bless.

Epilogue

Only God knows what the future holds for Pat and me.

However, as we look back over many years of following Him, we see tremendous blessing in every part of our lives. We have seen our family blessed, our business life blessed and the ministry He has given us blessed.

The key to this is obedience to God and walking carefully before Him. We should avoid sin at any cost. When God calls us to do something, we should obey. We can hear His voice as we read the Word of God every day and wait on Him in prayer. As we obey Him, He blesses and prospers us in every way.

Pat and I thank God for the wonderful health and strength He has given over the years and the way He has blessed our whole family. We would never want to go back to the way we were before we were born again.

As we look back over the last 21 years, we thank God for His goodness. We think of our grandson, Billy, who at eight years of age is leading young people of the same age to the Lord at church camps and is introducing them into the baptism with the Holy Spirit. "And a little child shall lead them."

When this life's journey is ended, we look forward to

being in His presence for eternity. We know of no greater gift that God could give us than to be with Him.

The marvellous thing is that it is so simple to receive eternal life. We do not need a theological degree. We do not need to strive and strain. We simply need to go on our knees, turn from our sins and ask Jesus Christ to come into our lives. As we fellowship with other Christians and read the Word of God and pray together, God will lead us day by day.

As the writer of Ecclesiastes says, "Remember your Creator before the silver cord is loosed, or the golden bowl is broken, or the pitcher shattered at the fountain, or the wheel broken at the well. Then the dust will return to the earth as it was, and the spirit will return to God who gave it." (Ecclesiastes 12:6-7).

Finally, he sums it all up perfectly, "Let us hear the conclusion of the whole matter: Fear God and keep His commandments, for this is the whole duty of man. For God will bring every work into judgment, including every secret thing, whether good or evil." (Ecclesiastes 12:13-14)

I have always remembered the words I learned in a little church so many years ago, "For what profit is it to a man if he gains the whole world, and loses his own soul? Or what will a man give in exchange for his soul?" (Matthew 16:26).

Even in my darkest moments, when I was so far from the Lord, I never forgot those words. Now Pat and I know that nothing this world can offer will ever approach being in the eternal presence and love of God.

Index